Expository Preparation

Expository Preparation

Preparing Your Soul to Preach

Benjamin G. Campbell

RESOURCE *Publications* • Eugene, Oregon

EXPOSITORY PREPARATION
Preparing Your Soul to Preach

Copyright © 2021 Benjamin G. Campbell. All rights reserved. Except for brief quotations in critical publications or reviews, no part of this book may be reproduced in any manner without prior written permission from the publisher. Write: Permissions, Wipf and Stock Publishers, 199 W. 8th Ave., Suite 3, Eugene, OR 97401.

Resource Publications
An Imprint of Wipf and Stock Publishers
199 W. 8th Ave., Suite 3
Eugene, OR 97401

www.wipfandstock.com

PAPERBACK ISBN: 978-1-6667-3023-4
HARDCOVER ISBN: 978-1-6667-2146-1
EBOOK ISBN: 978-1-6667-2147-8

08/30/21

To Rev. Timothy Campbell, my favorite preacher and role model, who raised me to love God and his Word.

Contents

Acknowledgements | ix
Introduction | xi

1. Biblical Authority: A Review | 1
2. The Pastor and the Spiritual Disciplines | 11
3. Preparation and the Pastor's Personal Life | 24
4. The Disciplines of Expository Preparation—Part 1 | 45
5. The Disciplines of Expository Preparation—Part 2 | 54
6. Preparation as Worship | 64
7. Basis for Worship | 75
8. Why Expository Preparation? | 81

Appendix 1: "The Role of Spirituality for Sermon Preparation and Delivery" | 87
Appendix 2: "Addressing Cultural Issues in the Pulpit: an Essay on Pastors as Public Theologians" | 106
Bibliography | 119

Acknowledgements

THE INITIAL WORK OF this project came through a portion of my seminary journey at Welch College. I spent many hours at the kitchen table with stacks of books and my Bible in hand. I could not have completed this project without the love and support of my family. To my wife, Kaylee, and sons, Beckett, and Haddon—thank you all for your invaluable support and love. It prodded me to continue and complete this project. I love you all more than you know!

A work like this is not complete without a rigorous edit. Sara Landing did such a wonderful job reading and rereading this manuscript. She was not only detailed in her revisions, but gracious in understanding the purpose of this work. Thank you, Sara, for your hard work.

Most of all, to the Lord Jesus– the One to whom all glory and honor is due—I pray my life will be an example and my preaching will be founded upon the union we share.

Introduction

"What is the process of preparation?" writes Martyn Lloyd-Jones on preparing to preach. "I would lay it down as a first postulate that he is always preparing. I mean that literally. That does not mean to say that he is always sitting at a desk; but he is always preparing."[1] You might read the previous quote and think, "Is preparation really all that necessary?" It is for this purpose that this book is written. I believe that the preparation of the pastor's soul is of *utmost* importance. If the pastor's soul is not in union with the Lord Jesus, he will have a difficult time shepherding the flock of God that is among him (1 Peter 5:2).

I know you are probably thinking it, so the question might as well be asked: Why another book on preaching? What will this book have to offer that hundreds, if not thousands, of other preaching books have not already conveyed? Hopefully, dear reader, you will see that this book has something within it to excite you and encourage you as you faithfully study and proclaim the Word of the living God. However, this book is ultimately not a work on preaching. It is, rather, a book on and for the pastor. You see, there have been many books written on the pastor and how he is to be a homiletician, exegete, and proclaimer of the truth of God's Word, but little to nothing has been written on the pastor himself.

---

1. Lloyd-Jones, *Preaching and Preachers*, 178.

Introduction

The Problem

For too long, preaching resources have been lacking a central focus in their composition. From correct exegesis to determining the best route of applying the text to those who will hear the sermon, most resources aim to aid the pastor in sermon construction. While sermon construction and homiletical techniques are important for preaching, the care of the pastor's soul is much more imperative. Even the most well-known books and resources regarding preaching deal more with the idea of preparing the sermon with homiletical skill instead of preparing the pastor to preach. Resources like Lloyd-Jones' *Preaching and Preachers*, Bryan Chapell's *Christ-Centered Preaching*, and Spurgeon's *Lectures to My Students* all deal with the construction and building of the sermon while only giving limited content, at best, to the preacher and his soul's care. Therefore, there is a need for expository preparation which entails different disciplines pertaining to the pastor's soul rather than refining his preaching skills.

A Massive Gap

The lack of adequate attention to such a topic results in a massive lacuna of resources regarding the pastor's soul. When the pastor's focus is solely on the sermon with little concern for his own soul, a void in sermon preparation becomes apparent. A chasm between soul and sermon is the cause of much ineffective preaching. Though preaching can be done without a pastor's soul being addressed throughout the preparation process, there is a biblical necessity for the consideration of the pastor's soul in his sermon preparation.

Therefore, pastors should follow Paul's instruction to Timothy when he said to "not neglect the gift you have, which was given you by prophecy when the council of elders laid their hands on you. Practice these things, immerse yourself in them, so that all may see your progress" (1 Timothy 4:14–15). If pastors are called

Introduction

to preach[2], they will (or should) strive to prepare their souls *and* their sermons well. Hence, preparing sermons effectively begins with the preparation of the pastor's soul, which must be the primary focus for his weekly tasks.

The Middleman

Since the pastor's aim must focus upon the preparation of his soul, he must regard the spiritual disciplines as the "middleman" of sermon preparation. The term "middleman" is used with foremost intentionality because the disciplines themselves connect the heart of the pastor to the text he aims to preach. Furthermore, they serve to also connect the pastor's heart to those who will hear the passage of Scripture interpreted, exegeted, and applied. Thus, the task of preaching sermons to a congregation from the sacred desk is a task that warrants the pastor's best work, which requires both soul preparation and public proclamation.

The Necessity for Pastoral Preparation

Since the middleman of the preparation of pastors and sermons is the spiritual disciplines, then these disciplines apply to the entirety of the pastor's life. Thus, the pastor's aim for excellence in the preparation of his sermons begins with his devotion to the Lord through the means of the spiritual disciplines. The spiritual disciplines establish the heart posture of the pastor through acts such as Bible intake, prayer, and meditation.

One's personal participation in the spiritual disciplines, then, is the necessary element needed for correct exegesis. Though correct exegesis is possible without a heart posture that is steered toward God, the application for such a passage of Scripture will be lacking without personal preparation and soul care. The absence

---

2. For a wonderful resource regarding the call to ministry, see Jason K. Allen's *Discerning Your Call to Ministry: How to Know for Sure and What to Do About It.*

Introduction

of such preparation stems from the emphases within a pastor's ministry in the local church—pastors might need to reorient their priorities.

The need for pastors to re-order their priorities has been noted in the study from LifeWay Research which says pastors who are overworked tend to prioritize their pastoral duties over their own spiritual growth and vitality.[3]

The re-ordering of a pastor's priorities begins with the foundation of his ministry, which is his union with Jesus Christ. Priorities in line with Scripture demand that the pastor's first and foremost priority to be the care of his own soul. Nothing is doable in Christian ministry without the power and strength of the Spirit within the pastor. Therefore, soul care is the most necessary priority every single day of the pastor's life—it is his lifeblood. Brother pastor, it is your lifeblood also.

So, when a pastor focuses his priorities *first* on his own soul, then biblical exegesis, application of the sermon, observing life (a term which will be defined later) with the congregation, and even his personal sanctification becomes a task worth working toward. Pastoral ministry and the task of preaching is a worthy task because the God who is working in and through the pastor does so to affect the hearers under the pastor's voice as he preaches.

A Significant Endeavor

This book, then, is an attempt to serve pastors with a foundation to not only biblical hermeneutics, but an attitude of worship and Christlikeness while preparing their souls and their sermons. Chapter one will present a review of biblical authority as a basis for what follows. Ultimately, no such sermon or the preparation thereof is possible unless the Bible is one's only authority. Then, the second chapter will correlate the pastor with the spiritual

---

3. According to LifeWay Research, 39% of evangelical pastors spend less than four hours per week in personal devotion to the Lord apart from their weekly teaching and preaching duties. See article entitled, "Pastor's Long Work Hours Come at the Expense of People, Ministry."

Introduction

disciplines to navigate a foundation for Christlikeness while sermon preparation is engaged. Once the pastor's spiritual life is healthy, only then can he move forward with his sermon preparation and prepare sermons. Sermon preparation begins with the pastor's soul and ends with his declaration from the sacred desk, while continually readdressing the holiness of his heart throughout the process. Chapter three will address the pastor's personal life: his rest, Sabbath, family time, and more.

After addressing the pastor's personal life, several disciplines are mentioned as necessary for the pastor to adequately prepare his sermons through. Chapters four and five address these disciplines, viewing them as disciplines *for sermon preparation*. Naturally, a person's spirituality begins with Bible intake, prayer, and meditation. However, once he acclimatizes these disciplines (that is, Bible intake, prayer, and meditation), one must go beyond the first step of soul preparation and look further into the pastor's sermon preparation, which will allow him to address his sanctification, interpreting the Bible rightly, recognizing theological themes within the passage, applying the selected text to his congregation, and being able to observe life with his congregation.

Chapter seven presents pastoral soul care as worship, followed by chapter eight which presents a biblical basis for worship in the church by addressing the final step of expository preparation—an analytical approach to viewing preaching as worship. Too often, pastors view the act of preaching as work rather than a divine means to proclaim the gospel in the stead of Christ himself. However, the more appropriate view of preaching is viewing it as the foremost element in worship—the essential aspect of the worship service. For preaching to be worshipful, it must be biblically based and theologically sound, and there must be an understanding that worship begins in the pastor's heart, not in the pulpit. Chapter nine will wrap up the book by explaining the necessity of expository preparation.

In the appendixes, I have also included two specific essays geared toward the pastor as he preaches. The first addresses the role of spirituality in both sermon preparation and delivery

Introduction

through the lens of the pastoral epistles. Paul said much to Timothy and Titus regarding their gifting, and pastors today can learn much from these letters. The second essay will address preaching through the lens of cultural involvement. Pastors are to be public thinkers and speakers, which means they are to be involved in culture. Sometimes, it can be difficult to discern what to say about cultural issues and when to say such things, which is the main reason for composing this essay.

This journey down a road of spirituality is a long and difficult one, beginning with sermon preparation, then shifting to sermon delivery. The Church, more than ever, needs pastors who are in deep, intimate communion with the Lord Jesus to lead His Church to health and vitality. Brother pastors, our main job is to proclaim the word of God. Therefore, we must do it with vigor, rigor, diligence, and integrity. I write this book not as an outsider, but as one who is right here in the trenches with you. If we want to see the gospel radiate and permeate through those God has entrusted under our care, we must prepare our souls well.

Benjamin G. Campbell
May 2021

1

Biblical Authority
A Review

THE QUESTION OF THE Bible's authority deals with two elements: inerrancy and revelation. To prove the truths of Christianity, the most popular method to do so is through the evidence.[1] However, is this the most beneficial method of proving God's existence? Ronald Nash claims otherwise and states, "Many philosophical and theological arguments are rejected, then, not because the person knows or believes that a particular premise is false, but simply because he fails to see something that others regard as obvious."[2] In other words, Nash seems to claim (a view with which I would agree) that certain "proofs" are more subjective than people might realize. For instance, the truthfulness of Christianity demands more from the one aiming to prove such a worldview; Christianity cannot *only* come from the evidence for God's existence, it must come from inerrancy and revelation.

Inerrancy and revelation are the two characteristics that aggregate to the authority of the Bible. It is not *only* that God's Word must be without error (though it is, because of the consistency

---

1. For a brief discourse on evidentialism, see John M. Frame's *The Doctrine of the Knowledge of God.*, 352–54.
2. Nash. *Faith and Reason*, 111.

and perfection of his personality), but also that what he speaks (or reveals) about himself must always be true because of who he is.

Inerrancy

Biblical inerrancy ultimately decodes itself in these propositions: God cannot err; the Bible is God's Word; therefore, God's Word cannot contain error.[3] Biblical inerrancy denotes itself by the character of God and the consistency of his nature; "All Scripture," Paul writes, "is breathed out by God" (2 Tim. 3:16).[4] Leroy Forlines exclaims that this is the only time in Scripture the Greek word *theopneustos* is used.[5] The testimony Paul makes to the nature of the Bible comes from the fact that the Scriptures (both Old and New Testaments) are God's literal words from his mouth—it is divinely breathed.[6] Hence, there is a propositional reality to the nature of inerrancy and revelation because God's truths are found through propositions in his Word. So, being that the Bible is God's inerrant words, one must assume, then, that what it contains within it is true and right by affirming propositional revelation.

Propositional Revelation

Propositional Revelation claims that the Bible is authoritative by its propositions contained within. However, the Bible is much more than only propositions—it is language, commands, exclamations, and more. Yet, all of these are made manifest through propositions.[7] In essence, propositional revelation does not claim that every jot and tittle is "inspired," but instead proposes the idea that Scripture is true and is coherent with reality because of the rational

---

3. Geisler, "Introduction and Bible", 248.

4. Unless otherwise noted, all biblical passages are referenced from *English Standard Version* (Wheaton: Crossway, 2001).

5. Forlines. *The Quest for Truth*, 43. (hereafter *Quest*)

6. Strong, *A Concise Dictionary of the Words in the Greek Testament and The Hebrew Bible*, 36.

7. Frame, *The Doctrine of the Knowledge of God*, 200–201.

and truthful nature of Creator God. So, then, propositional revelation deals more with the idea of the elements of the Bible's truth and how it applies to the life of a believer. This, again, is a direct correlation with inerrancy and infallibility.

The Chicago Statement and Its Effects

However, the discourse regarding the Bible's truth took a turn in the middle of the twentieth century when conservative, evangelical Christianity began to take progressive stances upon the inerrancy of Scripture, claiming that Scripture was not completely inerrant.[8] The summary of the *statement* extends the claim that Scripture is God's witness to himself.[9] However, the effects of the Chicago statement are more than mere questions about the Bible, but deal with how people (those claiming Christianity and not) deal with the questions of God's existence, God's authority, God's person, and God's character.

If the Bible is God's Word (which will be discussed further), then it *must* succeed that the Bible is coherent with reality. Therefore, a correct view of biblical inerrancy must be rooted in propositional revelation that applies to the theological method of believers in the Lord Jesus Christ.

Biblical Inerrancy in Light of Propositional Revelation

As noted earlier, biblical inerrancy necessitates itself in propositional revelation because the Bible is full of propositions through different elements of language and words. Carl Henry defines

---

8. For further study on the Chicago Statement, see Norman Geisler's *Defending Inerrancy: Affirming the Accuracy of Scripture for a New Generation*, 17–24. Geisler walks through the entire process of the International Council of Biblical Inerrancy: its founding, the construction of the statement, and more in this work.

9. "The Chicago Statement on Biblical Inerrancy," See http://www.bible-researcher.com/chicago1.html. (hereafter, *The Chicago Statement*)

propositional revelation helpfully by stating propositional revelation is the idea "that God supernaturally communicated his revelation to chosen spokesmen in the express form of cognitive truths, and that the inspired prophetic-apostolic proclamation reliably articulates these truths in sentences that are not internally contradictory."[10]

So, propositional revelation is not necessarily the fact that the Bible is inerrant because God is without error. God is, in his very nature, truth. It is not simply that God possesses truth, but he *is* Truth.[11] In other words, propositional revelation is dependent upon the nature and character of God,[12] and to do this, truth must be affirmed and believed also.

The Correspondence Theory and Propositional Revelation

The reality of inerrancy proves that truth and error are the core elements to whether the Bible is without error.[13] Put another way, the inerrancy of the Bible is contingent upon the nature of God and how God is truth, and that when he speaks, wills, and acts, his forthcoming actions are truthful and correspond with the way things are in the world. Ultimately, this is what it means to have a worldview, and Christians must ensure their worldview is biblically centered on truth and how it corresponds with reality. Therefore, the task of an evangelical is to analyze our current culture and fight the cultural relativism of postmodern thinking by adapting the correspondence theory of truth.

In its basic form, the correspondence theory claims that reality is what makes something true or false. Thus, a proposition is not made true simply because someone thought it; it must be determined by virtue of fact. Postmodern thinkers cannot assert

---

10. Henry, "The Bible as Propositional Revelation," 457.

11. Norman Geisler, "God and Creation," 356.

12. Before moving forward, I must note that this chapter is not for the purpose of establishing the existence of God. Instead, this serves to affirm the authority of the Bible through the reality of propositional revelation.

13. Geisler, *Defending Inerrancy*, 233.

such beliefs because they believe that truth is "a contingent of language."[14] As a result, the nature of truth for the postmodern worldview is only culturally embedded in its exclusive values and practices, not in facts that become a reality.

Therefore, the viewpoint of propositional revelation is such a valuable theory to believe because it proposes the notion that "the Bible is a propositional revelation of the unchanging truth of God."[15] For postmodernism, truth changes when culture changes which makes truth "anti-propositional" because it shifts when the society of the culture shifts. What follows, then, is the death of truth and reason.[16] So, it must be a necessity for Christians to believe in the notion of propositional revelation because of its unchanging nature that is transcended from the God who revealed himself by his words through human authors.

God's Word in Human Words

The consistent belief among evangelicals regarding inspiration is that God moved by his Spirit through human authors to pen the words of Scripture he sovereignly ordained to reveal about himself to humanity.[17] Because truth is the assembling of facts as they are experienced through reality,[18] one must understand the rationality and realistic nature of the Bible itself. The ultimate test of truthfulness of Scripture, again, is its correspondence with reality. So, regarding the Bible, one must seek to justify the Bible as truth rather than fairy tales, fables, or fiction. Hence, one does this in two different ways: affirming God as the ultimate truth-Giver and proposing the Bible as God's revealed Word.

The truth of God must be rationally interpreted through the lens of how truth is realized and understood. It is not sufficient

14. Ibid., 80.
15. Henry, *The Bible as Propositional Revelation*, 457.
16. Forlines, *Quest*, 26.
17. Ibid., 47.
18. Nash, *Life's Ultimate Questions*, 228.

to simply "prove" God's existence through a certain *apologetic argument* (as was previously noted in evidentialism), though these means can be sufficient to "prove" God's existence. Instead, a more fully orbed approach to ascertain the existence of God transpires through a pursuit of the knowledge of truth; essentially, he is the sovereign truth-Giver. The penultimate method for discovering truth is by properly understanding which particulars cohere in the best ways with reality. Some would argue that truth can be determined by each person individually, but this is not the case. Instead, truth must be justified belief.[19]

Justified Belief

Justified belief stabilizes itself in the notion that every person searches for truth with presuppositions. In other words, every person in the world has a way in which they view the world. Frame explains how one justifies a belief by a multitude of criteria: presuppositions, beliefs, and coherence with reality.[20] Ultimately, Christians do this as well, but it must be done through a Scriptural lens. The God of the Bible must be the foundation of truth to ascribe authority to his Word.

The Triune God has revealed himself to us by communicating within himself to humanity. The Father speaks to the Son, the Son speaks to the Father, and both to the Spirit and the Spirit to both.[21] Peter declares that "men spoke from God as they were carried along by the Holy Spirit" (2 Peter 1:21), so the process of the Bible being understood as God's Word begins with God revealing himself to the biblical authors by his Spirit, then succeeds to how the apostles witnessed the full revelation of God himself in the person of Jesus Christ. In principle, God is a communicator; therefore, God has communicated to humanity by his Word

---

19. For a more detailed study of knowledge and justified belief, see Frame's *The Doctrine of the Knowledge of God* and Plantinga's *Knowledge and Christian Belief*.

20. Frame, *The Doctrine of the Knowledge of God*, 104–22.

21. Frame, *The Doctrine of the Word of God*, 42.

through his relationship with humanity, and through Jesus Christ, the Incarnate Son.[22] Thus, God's truth is reality.[23]

Scripture as Authoritative

The view of Scripture as authoritative is a belief that transcends time—because God is eternal and ultimately, he is the Authority. However, the belief of biblical authority does more than make the Bible true, it makes it worth further study. That the Bible is only here to show us who God is limits the purpose of God's own revelation about himself. Thus, the Bible not only shows us who God is, but it also invites all who study it to apply its truths and propositions to daily life. God's authority is a product of his personality and character, therefore, whatever proceeds from his mind, heart, and will be authoritative because God cannot divorce his authority from his character.

Since God's character is embodied in his actions, this would include the revelation of himself to the world through his Word, Holy Scripture. In an article titled, "Hermeneutics and Biblical Authority,"[24] J.I. Packer presents seven different elements that make up the subject of biblical authority that are helpful for this discussion: inspiration, canonicity, self-authentication, self-sufficiency, clarity, mystery, and conscious submission. In this article, Packer declares that the basis of all biblical inspiration is Jesus Christ.[25]

The incarnation is not only the gracious work of God in Christ for salvation, but also a manifestation of the authoritative Word of God to the world (John 1:14). In the person of Jesus Christ, God's authority is realized by the way Christ lived: healing the sick, making the blind see, fulfilling the law (but not abolishing it), and ushering in the Kingdom of God. Jesus' claims to be God are only true if the authority is his, which is the case: "All authority

---

22. Forlines, *Quest*, 46.
23. Piper, *Expository Exultation*, 161.
24. Packer, "Hermeneutics and Biblical Authority."
25. Ibid., 8.

in heaven and on earth has been given to me" (Matt. 28:18). None of this is true unless God's Word is authoritative. "His authority is its, and its is His."[26]

In other words, the Bible's authority comes from the words revealed by God about God through God's Spirit to human authors who penned Holy Scripture. Everything God does is done out of love and grace, however, God also does nothing without authority. So, when God creates the world in Genesis 1, he not only seeks a relationship with the human beings he created, but he is also seeking to be their Lord and King. The same process happens, then, when one approaches the Bible. In grace and love, God has revealed himself to humanity through his Word, but none of his self-revelation is absent from his authority. Frame echoes, "when God speaks to rational beings . . . that meaning is authoritative. So, every page of the Bible teaches or illustrates the authority of God's word."[27]

A Necessary Foundation

In too many circles of evangelicalism, the denigration of the authority of Scripture is increasing. What began as seemingly unharmful discourse of differences, regarding the Bible and the character of God, turned into a diversion from truth. Henry notes, "In the secular university mood he," that is, Robert Johnston, "thinks seminary faculties should welcome major theological differences as long as the full authority of Scripture is professed."[28] This was the attitude of many evangelicals in the academy during the seventies and eighties, and it led many confessing conservatives to move toward progressive, liberal theology.[29]

---

26. Ibid., 11.
27. Frame, *The Doctrine of the Word of God*, 56.
28. Henry, "Evangelicals and Biblical Authority: A Review Article," 141.
29. While this is speculation upon my part, I do understand the necessity of biblical authority become a more prioritized issue during the conservative resurgence. All efforts during these times were to hold high the view of Scripture as authoritative and inerrant.

Biblical Authority

In summary, this is why a correct view of biblical authority, in light of propositional revelation, is necessary. Scripture reveals its own authority through its words and the interpreter must hold it to such a standard. Packer posits that unless we know how to determine what the Bible means, its authority is an empty notion.[30] Therefore, inerrancy is a requisite and the belief in propositional revelation is necessary to synthesize the notion of biblical authority through God's revelation of himself. Logically, biblical authority only works if the propositions in the Bible are directly from God. Again, it is not merely that every word is "inspired" (though conservative evangelicals would claim this, in some fashion). Instead, what we find is that logical consistency demands that in the propositions through which God has revealed himself, he expresses nothing but truth and exercises his authority. One author declares, "It is the revealed rather than the inspired characters which nowadays renders the Bible authoritative."[31]

However, the authority of Scripture being logically thought upon and meditated on is the crux of Christianity in general, in terms of epistemology. To determine what is true and false, one must either believe in the authority of the Bible or the lack thereof. The law of noncontradiction essentially claims that there is only once source of authority, and how can one ascribe authority with no precedent? It is impossible to ascribe authority unless one has eternal authority that manifests itself in human language and reasoning. This is the authority of the Bible—that God has manifested his authority through propositions in Holy Scripture. Though these propositions are sometimes vague and nuanced, they can be interpreted and understood with the help of the Holy Spirit, the third person of the Trinity.

The belief in biblical authority has massive ramifications for the pastor and his soul. If the Bible is reduced to mere theories, we "experience a strong temptation to imaging either that we do not really need the Bible to understand the natural world, or that it

---

30. Packer, *Hermeneutics and Biblical Authority*, 7.
31. Cave, "The Inerrancy of Scripture," 189.

plays at best a minor, incidental role."[32] Thus, propositional revelation is necessary for the Christian preacher because it necessitates the Bible as real facts rather than theories. Therefore, propositional revelation must precede conservative, Christian theological practices because it holds the Bible as factual reality rather than a theory *about* reality.

---

32. Poythress, *Redeeming Science: A God-Centered Approach*, 47.

2

The Pastor and the Spiritual Disciplines

THE LOCAL CHURCH HAS one goal: to proclaim the message of the gospel of Jesus Christ.[1] The God-ordained means by which the church is to proclaim the gospel is the preaching of the Word of God. Paul wrote to the Corinthians, "It pleased God through the folly of what we preach to save those who believe" (1 Cor. 1:21). Preaching should declare God's message to a gathered church for the purpose of salvation and sanctification. God uses ordinary men through ordinary means to communicate his divine message of salvation to the world. Bryan Chapell proffers the privilege of preaching when he states, "If your goal is Christ's honor you *can* be a great preacher through faithfulness to him and his message."[2]

This act of preaching is unlike any other task. In fact, it is a noble task (1 Timothy 3:1), and a task that allows the pastor to oversee what God has entrusted to him: his congregation (Titus 1:7). The most compelling way a pastor can lead his congregation is to expound upon the Scriptures faithfully. Preaching should be both the highlight and the most dreaded task of every pastor's week; Dan Doriani proffers that pastors should enter the pulpit in a mild state

1. Farrell, "Preach, Proclaim," 626.
2. Chapell, *Christ-Centered Preaching*, 32.

of panic.[3] The panic Doriani speaks of relates to the pastor and his preparation. Steven J. Lawson thinks similarly to Doriani by claiming that preaching is a paradoxical act because the pastor is both strong and weak.[4] In other words, the pastor may be strong in his skill of preaching, but in himself, he is unable to reach the hearts of those who sit under his preaching. Thus, the act of preaching only occurs through divine enablement by the Spirit of God.

If preaching is such a noble task, the pastor must take it seriously. Paul Bauermeister posits, "You are not being asked to try hard or to do your best. You are being asked to pledge yourself to faithfulness and holiness."[5] Moreover, to seriously consider his task, a pastor must be prepared to speak when he steps into the pulpit. This preparation begins and ends with the gospel of Jesus Christ. When pastors come into the pulpit, they must proclaim "It is finished!" not "Get to work."[6] Hence, the gospel message is not a message of behavioral modification, but that God, in his kindness and love, looked down on humanity in their fallen state and made a way for all to be reconciled back to a relationship with Him. If one is to speak about the wondrous mystery of the gospel, he must prepare thoroughly. Yet, preparation does not begin with the sermon itself, but with the pastor's soul.

In many circles of evangelicalism, hermeneutics can be the premier topic of discussion regarding preparation. Most writers today show favor toward the topic of correct exegesis.[7] However, a more careful examination of pastoral preparation through soul care is necessary.[8] Preparation of the sermon is, most definitely, essen-

---

3. Doriani, "Preach in a Mild State of Panic."

4. Lawson, *The Kind of Preaching God Blesses*, 73.

5. Bauermeister, "The Disciplines of Pastoral Formation: Habits Toward Holiness," 64–65.

6. Wilson, *The Pastor's Justification*, 121.

7. In reading works on preaching, there is little to nothing written on the pastor's soul. To assess the trend, see Brian Chapell's *Christ-Centered Preaching: Redeeming the Expository Sermon* and John MacArthur's *Rediscovering Expository Preaching*.

8. For further study on the pastor's soul, see Rick Reed's *The Heart of the Preacher: Preparing Your Soul to Proclaim the Word of God*.

tial but it is not the most fundamental part of sermon preparation. Instead of aiming solely for correct hermeneutics, the pastor should first prepare his own heart to preach. Lawson observes, "Our maturity is more important to Him than our ministry."[9] In other words, if the pastor's heart is not prepared to preach, it does not matter what is prepared to be communicated.

A pastor can prepare sermons, but unless his heart is in communion with the living God, his speech is nothing more than a speech. Communion with God means there is more to the pastor's soul than *only* salvation; it means he is pursuing Christlikeness. Therefore, a prerequisite for preaching is the necessity for pastors to prepare their hearts to preach by approaching the Bible like an animal searches for food. Matt Smethurst explains that there are some who will only "snack" on the Bible, but genuine Christians crave the bread of life for their daily source of nourishment.[10] The same is true of pastors; as pastors, there is a necessity to establish a pattern of holiness through the spiritual disciplines.

Preparation as Growth in Holiness

The pastor's preparation deals with the heart, and when a pastor considers his task, one finds that the preparation of the pastor is directly related to his spiritual life. To lead and preach for God's glory, the pastor must prepare his own heart; he must pursue holiness. "Pursue" is a necessary word that must be in place when speaking of holiness. The author of Hebrews writes that unless we strive for holiness and living peaceably with one another, we will not see the Lord (Heb. 12:14). Therefore, a personal pursuit of holiness is necessary for the pastor. A personal pursuit of holiness, for any believer, is mandated from Scripture to transform into the image of Christ (Rom. 8:29; 12:1–2), but this transformation does not happen because the pastor pursues holiness with adequate actions or with correct motives. Instead, it is given to us by grace that

---

9. Lawson, "Preparing the Pastor."
10. Smethurst, *Before You Open Your Bible*, 21–26.

allows these activities to mold them into godly beings.[11] Pastors could *aim* for holiness, but it would not be reachable without the grace of God given to them by God's Spirit.

In other words, simply *wanting* to be holy or *wishing* holiness upon oneself does not characterize someone as holy. Donald Whitney helpfully clarifies that holiness is not attainable unless we pursue it.[12] Without sincere pastoral concern for self-character development and soul care, there is no spiritual formation or growth. Thus, personal spiritual growth among pastors is necessary for three reasons.

First, the pastor's personal life depends upon it. The first reality is that pastors cannot pursue holiness unless they are a believer themselves.[13] Jesus clearly teaches that only those who know him can pursue him (John 10:27). Therefore, no one truly has a "spiritual" life until they are regenerated by the Holy Spirit. Nevertheless, the spiritual life of anyone (especially pastors) begins and ends with a rigorous pursuit of Christ himself.

This pursuit is necessary for those who profess Jesus Christ as their Savior because it demands they deny themselves, take up their cross, and follow him (Luke 9:23). Peter commands his readers to pursue Christ because he is soon to return, and Christians must be ready for his appearing (2 Peter 1:16–21). So, a pursuit of holiness encompasses one's entire life. However, the task of a pastor can often be weightier because God also entrusts a congregation under his care and leadership (James 3:1) that brings spiritual demands to such a task. Therefore, the pastor's soul care should be a top priority for himself and for his hearers (1 Tim. 4:16). Otherwise, ministerial repercussions may arise.

Second, the pastor's impact in the church depends upon his spiritual growth. A pastor's spiritual growth directly affects his influence within the local congregation he is leading. A pastor's

---

11. Emmert, "Resting in the Word of God: The Forgotten Spiritual Discipline," 37.

12. Whitney, *Spiritual Disciplines for the Christian Life*, 2. (hereafter, *Spiritual Disciplines*)

13. Pink, *Spiritual Growth*, 14.

influence comes from many different factors, but ultimately it pertains to his dealings with the congregation under his care, and from the application of his sermons. A pastor who does not know his people cannot adequately model spiritual growth. Otherwise, there can be no spiritual modeling or influence from his leadership. Murray Capill explains that pastors who are spiritually malnourished will often "be like a blockage in a pipe preventing water from flowing freely."[14] Modeling spirituality can only happen if a pastor is pursuing Christ himself.

In other words, it is possible to block the message of the gospel from flowing through the pastor to his congregation by neglecting the spiritual disciplines. Jesus asks the Father to keep his disciples through perseverance (John 17:11), but He also prays that those whom God has given him would be sanctified by the Word of truth and be one with the Father (John 17:18–21). This oneness with God reaches to the realm of pastors also. So, if oneness with God is absent, then there is no preparedness of one's heart to preach because there is no message to be funneled through the pastor's own heart and words to the congregation.

Third, the pastor's sermon preparation depends upon it. Ultimately, the pastor cannot adequately prepare to preach unless he is spiritually healthy, and spiritual health lies at the core of Christianity. To be spiritually healthy means that one is in constant relation with God through the spiritual disciplines prescribed in Scripture. If a pastor neglects to devote adequate time into the care of his soul, he can be guilty of "neglecting the gift of God that is in [him]" (1 Tim. 4:14).[15] Jerry Bridges summarizes that living for the Lord is the essence of what it means to be a disciple of Jesus.[16] Bridges agrees with Mark Dever's definition of discipleship when he says a person's discipleship is living a life of following Christ.[17]

The pastor's discipleship, then, should be his soul's foremost priority. Otherwise, preaching should not be an option for him.

---

14. Capill, *The Heart is the Target*, 82.
15. Bridges, *The Christian Ministry*, 194.
16. Bridges, *The Discipline of Grace*, 25.
17. Dever, *Discipling*, 14.

Paul writes to Titus that elders (pastors) should "hold firm to the trustworthy word as taught, so that he may be able to give instruction in sound doctrine and also to rebuke those who contradict it" (Titus 1:9). If a pastor is spiritually unhealthy, he is unfit to guide a congregated body of believers to spiritual health. Preaching while being spiritually unhealthy is hypocritical (2 Tim. 4:2), and spiritually unhealthy preaching is an oxymoron. Thus, it follows that a pastor's soul must be cared for him to simply prepare his own heart to preach. Else, there is a deficiency in the preparation of the sermon.

The Spiritual Disciplines Defined and Applied

Soul care is vital to every believer but is especially important to anyone who aims to pastor a local body of believers. The task of pastoring is more mental than physical, more emotional than impassive, and altogether spiritual. For this reason, a pastor must discipline himself for the purpose of godliness. However, before advancing to the definition and application of the disciplines themselves, a defining of terms is obligatory.

To many, the words "spiritual disciplines" can be a broad term, even a bit nuanced. Often, when people hear such words of which they have never defined biblically, the words end up being demarcated in a rather general sense. So, much care is needed to define the spiritual disciplines. Simply because one claims something to be "spiritual" does not make it a biblically warranted action of godliness. Don Carson asserts that our culture's perception of the spiritual disciplines defines them in ways of a "matter of technique" and a type of "self-flagellation" rather than something that is commanded from Scripture to grow us in holiness. He continues to proffer that the transformative component to spiritual disciplines is not in the discipline itself but in the value of what is being disciplined, i.e., "the value of prayer, the value of reading God's Word."[18]

---

18. Carson, "Spiritual Disciplines," 377–78.

The Pastor and the Spiritual Disciplines

What are the Spiritual Disciplines?

In short, the spiritual disciplines are "practices found in Scripture that promote spiritual growth among believers in the gospel of Jesus Christ."[19] They *are* in Scripture, meaning they are implicitly interwoven into the narrative of Scripture. Hardly ever does one read the Scriptures, specifically the Psalms, the Acts, and the Epistles, without finding a command to read the Scriptures and to devote oneself to prayer. The apostles in the church at Jerusalem were having trouble caring for their widows, so they instituted the office of the deacon so their pastors could "devote [themselves] to prayer and the ministry of the Word" (Acts 6:4). The apostles were understanding that the most important disciplines they could devote themselves to as leaders of the church were prayer and the ministry of the Word.

However, another important aspect to notice about the spiritual disciplines is that they are *practices*. Some might believe the spiritual disciplines are equivalent to the fruit of the Spirit (Gal. 5:22–23), but this is not the case. While the fruit of the Spirit is an outward expression of the Spirit's inward dwelling, the disciplines are practices—that is, acts of *being*—for believers in Jesus Christ to become like him (Rom. 8:29). Dallas Willard is correct by noting that discipline is the most significant part of the human soul's structure and that one cannot achieve anything without it.[20] Yet, discipline is not attained by casually approaching the Bible. Instead, it is only achieved when one pursues it to their fullest ability. In his commentary on the Psalms, John Phillips offers great wisdom to echo what Willard conveys. Phillips declares that you do not seek God with your whole heart (Ps. 119:10) if you only occasionally open your Bible.[21] Holiness is achieved when it is pursued through the discipline of spiritual habits.

---

19. Whitney, *Spiritual Disciplines*, 4.

20. Willard, "Spiritual Disciplines, Spiritual Formation, and the Restoration of the Soul," 106.

21. Phillips, "Psalms 89–150," 271.

Expository Preparation

Why Should Holiness Be Pursued?

The pursuit of holiness is why Paul urged Timothy to train (discipline) himself for godliness (1 Tim. 4:7). According to R. Kent Hughes, Paul is exhorting Timothy to experience some "spiritual sweat"[22] which would encourage Timothy to take on determination and diligence. A pursuit of holiness does not come naturally to a man; one must fight for its end. Hughes proffers, "Men, we will never get anywhere spiritually without a conscious divestment of the things that are holding us back."[23] Pastors can find themselves in spiritual slumps and the reason for a spiritual stagnation might be the neglect of the disciplines in a pastor's life; he no longer, as the psalmist writes, pants for God like a deer pants for water (Psalm 42:1). Neglect of one's union with Christ results in many pitfalls in ministry—spiritually, physically, mentally, and emotionally.

Although there is no specific chapter and verse that describes the disciplines, Scripture presents them implicitly in 1 Timothy 4 when Paul exhorts Timothy to take on practices, all resulting in godliness. It could be that Paul was encouraging Timothy to take on the attitude of Jeremiah when he prophesies, "Your words were found, and I ate them, and your words became to me a joy and the delight of my heart" (Jeremiah 15:16). Eugene Peterson paraphrases this same attitude very well in *The Message*: "What delight I took in being yours."[24] Delighting in being the Lord's is the essence of what it means to discipline for godliness. Then, the pastor's attitude becomes Jeremiah's, and he delights in the truth that he is God's, and God is his.

It is to this end the disciplines work within the pastor's life; they allow him the opportunity to know God. For example, one can logically conclude there is a God from the natural world (Rom. 1:20), but this conclusion only brings a knowledge that a creator exists; this knowledge does not allow one to *know* the Creator. The only means through which a person can know God is through his

---

22. Hughes, *Disciplines of a Godly Man*, 14.
23. Ibid.
24. Eugene Peterson, *The Message*.

communicating to us through his Word. If God is a communicator, then a couple of notions can be brought to attention. First, if God can be known, then, as his creation, we must pursue such knowledge. The Bible is clear that no one seeks after God apart from the Holy Spirit's drawing (Rom. 3:10; John 6:44). Second, if God can be known as a communicator, he must have given *means* by which humanity can know Him. The Bible, then, is God's message to *how* we can know him. John Piper says that if one wants to hear God speak, he must read the Bible aloud.[25] The Bible is the means through which God has chosen for those He created to know Him. Therefore, pastors must engage with the Bible to have communion with our Creator.

How Do the Disciplines Relate to Holiness?

The question of the relevance of personal holiness is the element that brings all elements together into a coherent whole. Jared C. Wilson asserts, "The pastor who neglects personal holiness has forgotten who's in charge."[26] However, J.I. Packer notes that one of the most neglected priorities in the Christian faith currently is the pursuit of holiness.[27] Therefore, one way holiness relates to the spiritual disciplines is to lessen the temptation for pastors to become legalistic in their personal pursuit of holiness. Hughes presents a wonderful comparison of how this plays out in a pastor's heart. He argues that legalism says, "I will do this thing to gain merit with God," but the disciplined heart says, "I will do this thing because I love God and want to please Him."[28]

You see, the way in which a pastor adequately pursues holiness is through a disciplined lifestyle in the Word and the ordinary means of grace given by God through which we know him. Joseph Harrod, in agreement with Michael G. Haykin, explains that the

---

25. Desiring God on Instagram accessed September 22, 2019, https://www.instagram.com/p/6h7KulSMnA/.
26. Wilson, *The Pastor's Justification*, 42.
27. Packer, *Keep in Step with the Spirit*, 81.
28. Hughes, *Disciplines of a Godly Man*, 15.

means of grace are prayer, the Scriptures, and the ordinances of Baptism and the Lord's Supper.[29] The means of grace are ordained to aid in the believer's pursuit of living a holy life and emulating Christlikeness to those around them. To this same end, the means of grace works for pastors. The ordinary means of grace plus the discipline that involves pursuing holiness is the only biblically warranted method to reach holy living.

The task of preaching, then, begins with the pastor's pursuit of holiness. How? Because it begins with the pastor's pursuit of knowing the God about which they are preaching. To spend time alone with God is, as Paul instructed Timothy, to immerse yourself in His Word (1 Tim. 4:15). Paul's instruction here relates to Timothy's moral progress in the Christian life, which can be interrelated to his own personal pursuit of holiness.[30] Once Timothy's pursuit of holiness was sure, only then could he begin to "save both [himself] and [his] hearers" (1 Tim. 4:16). The same is true for pastors who plan to stand behind a pulpit each week and proclaim the message of the gospel. There is no message worth preaching apart from the pastor's own interaction with the Holy Scriptures.

How Do the Disciplines Apply to the Pastor?

Pastors must apply the spiritual disciplines to their own lives for the purpose of adequately preparing their hearts to preach. Donald Whitney discusses such importance when he advises, "Don't settle only for spiritual food that's been 'predigested' by others."[31] In other words, *prioritize personal study before resorting to others' work*. Too often, pastors are diligent in studying books long before approaching the Bible. Instead of beginning their preparation with others' work, pastors should aim to immerse themselves in the Scripture to know God.

---

29. Harrod, "Knowing God from the Heart," 218.
30. Köstenberger, *Commentary on 1–2 Timothy and Titus*, 155.
31. Whitney, *Spiritual Disciplines*, 33.

The Pastor and the Spiritual Disciplines

If a pastor neglects personal holiness, he is neglecting Christ's presence in his life and in his ministry. The only foundation a pastor has in ministry, and especially his personal life, is Christ Jesus. Paul instructed Timothy to pay close attention to himself as it pertains to holiness because his hearers' spirituality depends upon it (1 Timothy 4:14–16). So, just as Paul is instructing Timothy to pay close attention to his own holiness so his hearers will be saved, the Holy Spirit is also instructing pastors through Paul's words to discipline themselves for godliness so their hearers will be saved in the pursuit. For the pastor to be disciplined, he must take on certain biblically warranted practices to aid in his pursuit of holy living.

Therefore, the most effective disciplines for pastors are Bible intake, prayer, and meditation. These three disciplines are the basic disciplines that align a pastor's heart with the Word of God. J. Oswald Sanders has much to impart to his readers concerning these disciplines. He declares, "The discipline is always a preparatory to blessing and can bring nothing but blessing when rightly received . . . Food not digested is a bane, not a blessing."[32] In other words, unless the daily bread is actually *digested* and not only chewed up and spit out, it is worthless devotion. Sanders' words relate to Isaiah's when he conveys that farmers do not continually plow; there are also stages of planting, nourishing, and harvesting their crops (Isaiah 28:23–29). The same is true when thinking of the way pastors read their Bibles, pray, and meditate on Scripture. If pastors are *only* "plowing," they will find their spiritual life in a circular motion going nowhere. Pastors must also impart their efforts to other stages of pursuing holiness. For this reason, the disciplines are necessary for the pastor's life and apply directly to his pursuit of holiness by showing him the importance of biblical centrality in every area of his life.

---

32. Sanders, *Spiritual Maturity*, 37.

Expository Preparation

Why are the Disciplines Important?

The spiritual disciplines are incredibly crucial for a pastor and sometimes, merely hearing the word "discipline" can be defeating. Discipline, however, is a powerful word pastors must define and apply carefully. The application spans to his family as it does his ministry: "If you are married, the presence or lack of spiritual disciplines can serve to sanctify or damn your children and grandchildren."[33] The presence of the spiritual disciplines, or lack thereof, can either help or hurt a pastor and his family. Not only can it play a part in determining his children's future, but it can also play a determining role in his personal life.

Pastors need the spiritual disciplines in place in their life to prepare their hearts to lead their congregations by preaching the Word of God—faith by hearing and hearing by the Word of God (Romans 10:17). Thus, pastors must take particular concern with the message they proclaim every week. Whitney helpfully clarifies that God does not save people *during* the preaching of the Word but *through* the preaching of the Word.[34] Therefore, the relevance of the disciplines cannot be over-emphasized to pastors who will stand behind the sacred desk each week and proclaim, "Thus saith the Lord."

Spiritual disciplines play a vital role in the pastor's preparation because they allow the pastor to pursue holiness for himself before he ever steps into the pulpit to herald the good news to those under his care and watch. Paul writes to the Corinthians that though the outer self is fading away, the inner self is being renewed day by day (2 Cor. 4:16), but also to be renewing our minds daily (Rom. 12:2). This renewal comes from the pursuit of holiness, a pursuit of God himself. John Piper explains that this inner renewal of our minds is for the purpose of embodying the glory of God for those around us to see.[35]

---

33. Hughes, *Disciplines of a Godly Man*, 16.
34. Whitney, *Spiritual Disciplines Within Your Church*, 67.
35. Piper, *A Peculiar Glory*, 144.

The Pastor and the Spiritual Disciplines

This embodiment should be the mission of every Christian, for Christ has commanded as much: "Let your light shine before others, so that they may see your good works and give glory to your Father who is in heaven" (Matt. 5:16). The light that shines to a pastor's congregation is the illumination of God's Spirit within him, through a union with Jesus Christ, the Son. The fruit of the pastor's efforts to discipline himself for godliness will most likely be unseen in his lifetime, but he will be rewarded for his faithfulness on the last day. This was Paul's wish, and it should be the pastor's also, to "keep the faith" (2 Tim. 4:7) as he disciplines himself to lead a congregation to spiritual vitality through communion with Jesus Christ, our Lord.

3

Preparation and the Pastor's Personal Life

THE PASTOR MUST HAVE a steady hold on his personal life if he is to be sufficiently prepared to preach. Only taking care of a sermon construction does not suffice as taking care of one's soul because one cultivates maturity through the inner self.[1] Therefore, a pastor must take an honest examination of his Christian life and follow the Lord Jesus all the days of his life to focus on his soul's maturity. This maturation process comes through a variety of different means. Thus, pastors must understand that to truly mature as shepherds in the Church of God; they must love the God of which they preach. Nevertheless, the only way to develop a love for God is to devote oneself to Him through the spiritual disciplines, which will then lead to the pastor preaching only what he loves, Christ Jesus and him crucified (1 Cor. 2:2). Lewis Allen posits, "You can only preach what you love. One can only truly love if they know God and feed daily by His Word. God is always preaching himself as the God of love. He has no greater message, no other gospel, and no greater purpose. Neither do we."[2]

---

1. Gibson, "The Preacher's Personal World," 54.
2. Allen, *The Preacher's Catechism*, 30.

Therefore, the pastor must aim to love the God upon which he bases his sermons. However, one cannot love God unless he pursues Him through a union with His Son.

The Devotional Life of the Pastor

The writer to the Hebrews exclaims that the Lord disciplines us to "share his holiness" (Heb. 12:10). Here the author explains to his audience (likely Jewish Christians)[3] that there is no such thing as enjoyable discipline, but it "yields the peaceful fruit of righteousness to those who have been trained by it" (Heb. 12:11).[4] The process of sanctification is, in fact, a progressive process throughout the entirety of life. It is, as Jerry Bridges so helpfully defines, a lifetime of "likeness to our Lord Jesus Christ."[5] Paul conveyed this idea in the letter to the Romans that God is working all things for our good, in order that we might "be conformed to the image of his Son" (Rom. 8:29). This process of sanctification is ordained by God to change our likeness into Christ's. Every Christian's goal should be to pursue a life of Christlikeness for the glory of God.

Therefore, the pastor's pursuit of Christ and his likeness is essential to his preparation. A pastor must be intentional about his habits to discipline himself for godliness. Habits are necessary for the Christian life because they not only result in godliness (when practiced regularly) but because building habits in life is necessary to our happiness.[6] These habits come through three main areas of devotion to God: Bible intake, prayer, and meditation of Scripture.

---

3. This view is presented by a majority of New Testament scholars. For a well-thought study of the destination and addressees, see Thomas R. Schreiner's "Commentary on Hebrews,", 7.

4. Referenced from the *Christian Standard Bible* (Nashville: B&H, 2017).

5. Bridges, *The Discipline of Grace*, 100.

6. Duhigg, *The Power of Habit*, 48–50.

Expository Preparation

The Bible Intake of the Pastor

John Wesley believed that the most crucial component for one's rule of doctrine, practice, and experience was the Bible itself.[7] The Bible is the means through which one grows into Christlikeness over their lifetime. Therefore, the pastor must render the Word of God right, precise, and sufficient. In Psalm 119, the psalmist delighted in the law of the Lord (verses 14; 16; 24; 35; 47; 70; 77; 92; 143; 174), he never strayed from keeping the Lord's precepts (v. 4), his heart was satisfied beyond all riches (v. 14), he is counseled through the Word (v. 24), and even while the psalmist's enemies were waging against him, he was delighting in the Lord and His Word (v. 70).

The pastor's desire must be that of the psalmist's: to delight in the law of the Lord. However, to delight in the Lord, the pastor must seek the Lord with the totality of himself (Ps. 119:10). Just as half-hearted commitment results in a lack of devotion, a lackadaisical seeking of the Lord results in a sluggish faith and, more importantly, idle soul care. Therefore, it is vitally essential for those who preach to understand the magnitude of being disciplined by personal interaction with the Word of God. Not only was Wesley living with the Bible as his standard of livelihood, but he was also adamant to read the Bible, pray, and meditate upon the words of Scripture in the context of his prayers daily.[8] This attitude should be manifested within the soul of the pastor as well, and a pastor's Bible intake is one of the most critical facets through which this attitude becomes a reality.

Paul wrote to Timothy to "bring the cloak that I left with Carpus at Troas, also the books, and *above all the parchments*" (2 Tim. 4:13, emphasis mine).[9] Although there is a large amount of

---

7. Affleck, "John Wesley's Spiritual Disciplines for Today's Pastor," 2.

8. Ibid.

9. Köstenberger notes that these parchments might have contained portions of Scripture, or possibly even the final drafts of his epistles. Either way, these documents were important to Paul and, I would argue, most likely contained *some* Scriptural content within, all of which were vitally important to the apostle. See Köstenberger, *Commentary on 1–2 Timothy and Titus*.

speculation regarding Paul's meaning when he writes about the parchments, it is highly likely that there was at least a portion of Scripture contained within them. Pastors should aim for the same devotion through their intake of God's Word. In other words, the Word of God is given through different forms to intake such truth. Of course, there must be a priority of Bible study, but other forms of study are necessary as well for the Christian mind. Hughes submits, "You can never have a Christian mind without reading the Scriptures regularly because *you cannot be profoundly influenced by that which you do not know.*"[10] So, to truly possess a Christian mind that engages with the world through the lens of biblical authority and gospel centrality, pastors must engage themselves with the Bible in a similar way to that of Paul and John Wesley.

Jesus himself was devoted to studying, living, and modeling the Bible in his own life, and one would be amiss to neglect the model of the Lord Jesus in these disciplines. The gospel of Luke records that Jesus "increased in wisdom and in stature and in favor with God and man" (Luke 2:52). Les Hardin conveys, "Jesus' knowledge of Scripture was not downloaded Matrix-style into his consciousness."[11] Thus, one must pay close attention to the life of Christ to find a "method" for discipling themselves for Bible intake. Donald Whitney agrees and declares that if people want to hear and learn the Word of God, they must discipline themselves to do as much.[12]

If laypeople are to discipline themselves to hear and learn the Word, then pastors are that much more required to do so. This demand to discipline is indeed biblically rooted in several passages of Scripture, but a clear mandate is in John's account of the ministry of Jesus. He records, "Abide in me and I in you. As the branch cannot bear fruit by itself, unless it abides in the vine, neither can you, unless you abide in me" (John 15:4). Of course, a branch that is grafted onto the vine that does not bear fruit is "thrown away" and "thrown into the fire and burned" (John 15:6). The disciples

10. Hughes, *Disciplines of a Godly Man*, 77.
11. Hardin, "The Quest for the Spiritual Jesus," 223.
12. Whitney, *Spiritual Disciplines*, 24.

Expository Preparation

had no idea that such a branch was among them in the person of Judas Iscariot, but the truth of verse 6 remains certain. Therefore, for pastors to prepare well, they must abide in the vine of Christ, and one way to accomplish this is through daily immersion in the Bible as one's bread of life.

Pastors are not to be like Judas Iscariot, i.e., those who fool everyone around them into thinking they are abiding in Christ. Pastors do not have room in their ministries for trickery, especially when it comes to preaching. Eventually, their trickery will manifest itself because what people believe and value is what they will express through action.[13] This trickery will, then, eventually come through how one preaches, and, consequently, will begin to creep into how a pastor prepares himself to preach. When preparation is fraudulent, so is the pastor's spirituality because pastoral preparation to preach is all about soul care.

If pastors continue down a path of neglect regarding their soul care, they will eventually become a poison to their congregations. Even healthy foods can be manipulated and made unhealthy. Sugar can be added to fruit and it can be fried, completely ruining the healthiness of the original food. Nevertheless, many pastors do this each week when they neglect their soul and preach each week; they ruin the content of the gospel by neglecting to prepare their own heart to preach God's divine revelation and truth. Thus, it dilutes their message to mere moralism and self-help principles rather than biblical truth, which leaves the pastor's congregation starving for spiritual nourishment.

R.C. Sproul explains that this is not the command Jesus gave Peter. Jesus did not command Peter to entertain or give His church self-help principles; he said to "feed *His* sheep" (John 21:17, emphasis mine). He writes, "Undershepherds feed the sheep because they feed with them on the Great Shepherd, whose flesh is food indeed."[14] However, feeding the sheep also entails how a pastor prays for himself and his hearers.

---

13. Freeman, "The Spiritual Disciplines in Personal Formation," 94.
14. Sproul, "A Pastoral Preeminence: Feed My Sheep," 41.

Preparation and the Pastor's Personal Life

The Prayer Life of the Pastor

Sinclair Ferguson suggests that a person's spiritual life is resourced through their communion with Christ as the source of *their* life.[15] Believers in Jesus Christ have an "all-access pass" to the Father because of their Great High Priest, who sacrificed himself so we can boldly approach the throne of grace (Heb. 4:14–16). John Calvin exhorted his readers to understand that, when they approach the Lord in prayer, they are not approaching an abstract idea, but are "entering into converse with God."[16] Prayer, as it pertains to the preparation of the pastor, deals with the pastor's conversing with God. Therefore, pastors must converse with God regarding two specific areas.

First, pastors must pray regarding themselves. If a pastor is to be adequately prepared to preach once he reaches the pulpit, it will require substantial, intentional prayer during the week leading up to Sunday. In his work, *On Pastoring*, H.B. Charles charges his readers (mainly pastors) with the notion that if they strive for effective ministry, they should be mentally prepared and concentrated, but also be spiritually devoted.[17] Prayer is an essential aspect of this mental preparation and concentration. Prayer is also the most necessary element to spiritual devotion, other than Bible intake, and the pastor must be on a constant knee in prayer throughout the week. It expresses his dependence upon the Lord for faithfulness and fruitfulness.

Second, pastors must pray for their congregation. It should be no surprise that pastors are to pray for those under their care. Because shepherding the flock of God relates to soul care, it follows that the first step in congregational soul care is intercessory prayer for those in the congregation with which a pastor is entrusted. Mark Dever notes that becoming acquainted with your

---

15. Ferguson, *Maturity*, 35.
16. Calvin, *Institutes of the Christian Religion*, 565.
17. Charles, *On Pastoring*, 152.

Expository Preparation

congregation to pray for them can be a powerful way to grow your influence as a pastor in your local church.[18]

However, there is a third necessity when it comes to the pastor's devotional life that must be included in the pastor's regular devotional habits: biblical meditation.

The Meditation of Scripture in the Life of the Pastor

As human beings, our minds are encompassed with things that bring us the most delight. For many, these delights come in the form of their job, finances, family, or other things. However, the psalmist declared that his delight was in the Word of God (Ps. 1:2).

Of course, meditation of the biblical text is more than merely reading and thinking about it for a while. Biblical meditation is not a simple thought that comes to mind and *reminds* us of Bible verses.[19] Instead, biblical meditation is achieved when one takes biblical passages and thinks deeply regarding the spiritual truths entailed within.[20] Thus, instead of meditation being an act of relaxation or a means to rid oneself of distraction, it is a spiritual act in which a believer in Jesus Christ can seek to grow in his union with him.

In other words, the cause of a lack of meditation in one's life could be that the pastor is not sitting down long enough to think about what the biblical text is saying. Often in this busy world, pastors have no time to sit in silence and consider (that is, meditate on) the depth of truth they are absorbing through prayer and Bible intake. Thus, silence and solitude could be a solution to the pastor's meditational habits. Robert Plummer writes, "Silence is complete quiet for spiritual purposes. Solitude is complete aloneness for spiritual purposes."[21]

---

18. Dever and Alexander, *The Deliberate Church*, 36.

19. For a devotional study of biblical meditation, see Robert J. Morgan's *Reclaiming the Lost Art of Biblical Meditation: Find True Peace in Jesus*.

20. Whitney, *Spiritual Disciplines*, 46.

21. Plummer, "Are the Spiritual Disciplines of 'Silence and Solitude' Really Biblical?," 102.

Preparation and the Pastor's Personal Life

Silence and solitude would benefit the pastor greatly as he prepares his heart to preach because it would allow him to meditate on the Scriptures without distractions. Thus, one of the leading causes of failed meditation is the lack of time our minds focus on a specific truth or passage we have examined. Donald Whitney likens this to coming in from a snowy and cold winter night and seeing a crackling fire only to take your gloves off and rub your hands together for warmth. However, as you are warming your hands, you realize that you are *still cold* because you are across the room from the fire. The problem is not you, but your method of warming yourself.

Moreover, the same is true in our endeavors of meditation. We often find ourselves failing to linger around the fire long enough to warm ourselves by the fire of God's Word.[22] When approaching the Bible for meditation, a pastor must first immerse himself in Scripture, pray himself clear, and this will enable the Scripture to permeate his soul to meditate on the truths contained in the Word. However, the devotional life of the pastor is only the first step in preparing himself to preach. This is the basis for his spiritual life—disciplines leading the pastor to spiritual health and flourishing.

The spiritual disciplines are necessary for the pastor to continue developing a love for God and growth in holiness. This love for Christ and growth in holiness comes through the pastor's devotional life, but another vital aspect of the pastor's soul care in his preparation to preach is his prayer life.

The Prayer Life of the Pastor

While prayer can come in the form of one's devotional life, as mentioned above, it is not limited to as much. Prayer is also a lifelong action for those who are children of God—it is the way of communication between the Creator and his creation. Prayer is not merely a necessity or a command, although it is such things; it is a

---

22. Whitney, *Spiritual Disciplines*, 49.

way of life.[23] For the pastor, therefore, prayer is not only a way to devote himself to God, but it is a way of life for him—it is a portion of his pastoral task. A pastor can implement prayer in his life in three different ways.

The Personal Prayer Life of the Pastor

Paul repeatedly encouraged the churches he planted to pray without ceasing (1 Thess. 5:17) and to continue steadfastly in prayer (Col. 4:2); however, he also conveyed to these churches that he remembered them in his prayers (2 Cor. 1:11), and that praying for his brethren was the source of his joy (Phil. 1:3–4). Paul's prayer life was never abolished because of his suffering, nor should the pastor's personal prayer life be absent from his life because of circumstances. Thus, a pastor should prioritize his personal prayer life for the following reasons.

First, the health of his soul depends upon his prayer habits. Prayer is the ultimate responsibility of the Christian life. Rick Reed explains that a failure to pray is a failure of soul care.[24] Jesus gave us the ultimate need for prayer when he told his disciples, "Apart from me you can do nothing" (John 15:5). Just as the disciples cannot do anything apart from the Spirit of God living within them, neither can pastors do anything for the Kingdom of God without the power of the Spirit, which is accessed through a personal prayer life.

Second, his sermon preparation is dependent on his vibrant prayer life. Prayer regarding the sermon should be a natural outflowing of the pastor's personal prayers. Because a majority of the pastoral task is preaching, it follows that a pastor must be continually active in praying for the sermon he will preach on the upcoming Sunday. For instance, Piper notes, "A cry for help from the heart of a childlike pastor is sweet praise in the ears of

---

23. Whitney, *Spiritual Disciplines*, 83.
24. Reed, *The Heart of the Preacher*, 135.

God."[25] Likewise, Spurgeon also claims that a genuine minister of the gospel will be one that utters a petition as arrows in the sky.[26] In other words, pastors should be people of prayer because a faithful preacher is a rigorous pray-er.[27]

Third, what is in the well is what comes up in the bucket.[28] Preaching and pastoring are only done effectively through prayer. Pastors are not so talented and skilled that their dependence can be self-fulfilled—their dependence must always be on the Lord Jesus. Joel Beeke claims that the Church is in desperate need of preachers who exemplify their prayer lives and bring them to light in the pulpit through their sermons.[29] However, more important than anything else is the posture of the pastor's heart. The question is not if the pastor prays in the morning before everyone else, but whether he prepares his heart to commune with the Creator of the universe.[30] In other words, the proper posture of a pastor's heart is not determined by the number of his prayers, but the extent of his communion with the Lord through his prayer life.

The personal prayer life of the pastor must take precedence over every other pastoral activity. The reason for such primacy is because prayer is an essential element to a pastor's ministry. However, a pastor's personal prayer life is not the only way in which he should pray. He should also prioritize his family and their centrality around the gospel of Jesus Christ.

The Familial Prayer Life of the Pastor

Not only is the pastor's prayer life an absolute necessity in the preparation to preach, but the pastor's familial prayer life must be prioritized. Paul declared that pastors should manage their

---

25. Piper, *Brothers, We Are Not Professionals*, 70.
26. Spurgeon, *Lectures to My Students*, 42.
27. Reed, *The Heart of the Preacher*, 135.
28. Charles, *On Pastoring*, 153.
29. Beeke, *Reformed Preaching*, 81.
30. Hughes, *Disciplines of a Godly Man*, 104.

household well (1 Tim. 3:4) and that they should also have families who are believers in Jesus Christ (Titus 1:6). This can cause a conundrum for some because it brings up the question of wayward children or spouses. However, most of these issues could be solved if the pastor would not neglect to shepherd his household before he shepherds the local congregation under his leadership. Kent Hughes posits that men have the power (influence) within their own respective families to steer their children toward godliness.[31]

Children naturally take their habits and mannerisms from their parents. So, if the pastor spends his time at home allowing his children (and even his wife!) to see him praying, his family will begin to view prayer as essential and necessary.[32] Family prayer should be a priority in every Christian household, but especially in the pastor's home. It should not be a time where everyone is forced to pray (Eph. 6:4), nor should it be a time when prayer is meaningless (Matt. 6:7). Instead, this should prompt us, as fathers and husbands, to make family prayer a time of joy and purpose for a familial communion with the Lord. The persevering aspect of family devotions and prayer can yield godly fruit in the pastor's family.

However, the activity of such prayer within the family is no easy completion. It takes determination and boldness with one's spouse and children. Family prayer is hard work, but the hardest things in life are the things that often yield the most fruit. Fernando explains that in order for children to be cared for, the parents must be healthy and strong.[33] The health and strength come from a heart that is spiritually prepared to do such things. Nevertheless, much like preparing to lead their family, a pastor must also be spiritually healthy to lead the church with which he has been entrusted.

---

31. Hughes, *Disciplines of a Godly Man*, 47.
32. Fernando, *The Family Life of a Christian Leader*, 28.
33. Ibid., 106.

Preparation and the Pastor's Personal Life

The Pastoral Prayer Life of the Pastor

Charles Bridges writes, "The greatest and hardest preparation is within."[34] If a pastor is to prepare himself to preach, he is also preparing himself to pastor, for preaching is a vital aspect of pastoring. The pastor's prayer life begins within himself, then extends even to the members of those under his leadership and shepherding. As described earlier in this book, prayer is not a simple task; it takes courage and discipline. Martyn Lloyd-Jones advises that before a pastor prays at all, he must first know himself. The problem is not *necessarily* in the fact that pastors *neglect their prayer life in their pastoral calling*, but that they *are not doing it in a way that yields the best results*.[35] Bill Hull notes that the sad reality is that many pastors in the West have bred a pushback against discipline, which has resulted in its neglect altogether.[36] When pastors speak negatively about discipline (in any form), it will breed neglect of it altogether, which will result in a digression of spirituality within the pastor's life if done for extended lengths of time.

Only behind his personal prayer life and the familial prayer life, the pastor's pastoral prayer life should be a top priority for his ministry. The pastorate can often become immensely busy with the daily requirements of the task at hand. However, when we examine the biblical accounts of the apostles, specifically in the book of Acts, we find that they devoted themselves to prayer and the Word (Acts 6:4). Don Carson wisely points out that if pastors are too busy to pray, they must cut something out of their schedules to make time for prayer.[37] Jesus rebukes Martha for being too busy worrying about the little mundane things in the house rather than the presence of God, the Son, in her living room, all while Mary is focusing on the presence of the Lord Jesus in her house (Luke 10:41–42). Sadly, this is the reality of many pastors in evangelical

---

34. Bridges, *The Christian Ministry*, 62.
35. Lloyd-Jones, *Preaching and Preachers*, 181.
36. Hull, *Conversion and Discipleship*, 134.
37. Carson, *A Call to Spiritual Reformation*, 114. (hereafter, *Spiritual Reformation*)

Christianity today. Pastors are too busy worrying about methods and structures to get people into their church that they neglect to pray to the Lord of the Harvest to bring forth fruit (Matt. 9:35–38). Thus, they should have the attitude of Mary, who ignored the busyness of her life to sit down with the Master and learn from him.

Therefore, the pastor is not dismissed from the activity of prayer because he is called to the gospel ministry. Spurgeon argues that a pastor who does not pray regularly is not qualified for the ministry in the first place; he also notes that biblical texts will often be meaningless until the keys of prayer open them.[38] Carson agrees with Spurgeon and asserts, "From God's perspective, such Christians are 'adulterous people' (Ja. 4:4), because while nominally maintaining an intimate relationship with God, they are trying to foster an intimate relationship with the world."[39]

Therefore, pastors are to be men whose lives are devoted to the ministry of personal, familial, and pastoral prayer. Furthermore, directly related to the prayer life of the pastor is how a pastor prepares himself through his study, spiritually and intellectually, to preach.

The Study Habits of the Pastor

The study habits of the pastor indicate the health of his spiritual life. Therefore, the pastor needs to pay close attention to these three areas of study: his personal study, his sermonic study, and his intellectual study.

The Personal Study of the Pastor

Pastors are continually interacting with the Bible through sermon preparation, counseling, pastoral visits and care, and in other areas. Thus, it may seem as though personal Bible study could be just another *task* to complete. Therefore, pastors should guard against

---

38. Spurgeon, *Lectures*, 42–43.
39. Carson, *Spiritual Reformation*, 121.

making Bible study a mere addition to their work calendars. Martyn Lloyd-Jones advises that pastors ought to read Scripture for more than the purpose of finding passages of Scripture for sermons.[40] A pastor with such engagement in Scripture is in grave error and danger spiritually. This is not to claim that sermons cannot come from one's personal reading of Scripture—the Word of God can work in this way—but that reading the Bible should never be for the sole purpose of finding a text to preach.

If a pastor is to be transformed into the image of Christ, it will be through a disciplined life in communion with God. Therefore, a pastor must discipline himself to take time for his personal growth. This personal growth is the way he fills his reservoir. A pastor cannot fill his reservoir unless he is taking the time to nourish himself with the Word of God. Hence, taking time to nourish oneself requires intentionality and commitment that only comes from making time for such activities. Lloyd-Jones advises pastors to "safeguard their mornings," so they will not be distracted and neglect to prepare for their work in the pulpit.[41]

In his book, *Ten Questions to Diagnose Your Spiritual Health*, Donald Whitney offers a question that all pastors should ask themselves on a weekly (possibly daily) basis: "Do you thirst for God?"[42] This is an essential question for a pastor's personal Bible study. The psalmist claims that God "satisfies the longing soul" (Ps. 107:9). However, God does not satisfy the longing soul with something other than himself.[43] Thus, a pastor must always be thirsting for God, and this satisfaction is only achieved through a personal Bible study.

However, a personal Bible study is not the only element of study in which a pastor must add to his weekly tasks. Thus, a pastor must also make time to study well for his sermons.

---

40. Lloyd-Jones, *Preaching and Preachers*, 184.
41. Ibid., 179.
42. Whitney, *Ten Questions to Diagnose Your Spiritual Health*, 15–28.
43. Ibid., 24.

Expository Preparation

The Sermonic Study of the Pastor

Pastors can often find themselves in time crunches during their week either from neglect to discipline themselves for the task, or from other pastoral duties taking precedence. Lack of time can often prompt a pastor to place his sermon(s) farther down on his list of priorities making his sermons less important than other pastoral duties. Therefore, because of a lack of time and misplaced priorities, pastors will often resort to a sermon from years past that has been preached before, or they will resort to putting inadequate amounts of time into studying.

However, another problem that can arise from a lack of prioritization is preaching someone else's sermon. Scott Gibson writes, "A responsible preacher does the majority of his or her work, possibly stimulated by various preaching resources, and prays to God for wisdom, guidance, and discernment."[44] This problem of preaching someone else's sermon entails more than the sin of stealing someone else's material, but it deals with the pastor's heart condition. A pastor who is consistently neglecting to preach and prepare his own sermons is one who consistently neglects his holiness. In other words, unless a pastor immerses himself in the Word of God, he is not preaching his own sermon. Therefore, the pastor must prioritize his content toward Scripture, *then* the use of other resources.[45]

Nevertheless, a pastor's sermon study could be considered a spiritual discipline because it is directly related to prayer when done biblically. According to Wesley Allen, a typical Jew would honor an hour of study as an hour of prayer.[46] In other words, an hour of sermon preparation could be considered an hour of prayer because it is communing with God to proclaim his Word to his people. This becomes a discipline because sermon preparation can often be neglected from laziness or other priorities. So, for a pastor to prepare well, he must study well for his sermons.

---

44. Gibson, *Should We Use Someone Else's Sermon?*, 69.
45. Campbell, "Preparing the Sermon," 147.
46. Allen, "An Hour of Study," 28.

Preparation and the Pastor's Personal Life

Just as studying for a sermon should be a top priority of the pastor's week, so should the pastor's mind be a priority throughout his life. A pastor should not only be concerned with his sermons but should also be concerned with the knowledge of which he possesses and always acquiring more.

The Intellectual Study of the Pastor

Paul wrote to the Romans that we ought to transform into the image of Christ by renewing our mind (Rom. 12:2); Jesus added to the Great Commandment to love the Lord with all our minds (Matt. 22:37). Therefore, the pastor must be continually learning. To correctly model what it means to follow Christ, the pastor must be a disciple—that is, he must devote his life to learning. Thus, a pastor should commit himself to learning in at least three ways.

First, a pastor can learn by studying theology. Theology must play a vital role in the soul care of the pastor, but also it must play a vital role in his preparation, for the Bible is theology. Martyn Lloyd-Jones explains the importance of pastors to study theology when he advises those under his teaching to read theology until they die, because being a theologian does not stop once you attain a degree.[47] Pastors need theology to lead the church well. Of course, not only is theology of the church necessary; likewise, systematic theology, biblical theology, practical theology, and others are necessary for the pastor to shepherd his congregation because theology and spirituality are inseparable.[48]

Second, a pastor can learn by reading Christian biographies. Biographies benefit the pastor in a couple of different ways. On the one hand, they allow the pastor to be well read with the "greats" of the Christian faith. On the other hand, it allows the pastor to interact with church history to a certain extent. Reading biographies of Luther, Calvin, Edwards, and others will allow the pastor to establish and understand the truth that history does repeat itself,

---

47. Lloyd-Jones, *Preaching and Preachers*, 188.
48. McGrath, *Mere Discipleship*, 116.

even in the church. In essence, pastors must understand that in every situation, the church has experienced the same difficulties, and reading biographies allows him to see how others in the same situation handled specific issues. As Piper notes, this gives the pastor an opportunity to "guard us against chronological snobbery (as C.S. Lewis calls it)."[49]

Third, a pastor can learn by reading other genres. While the reading of theology and biographies are vitally important components of pastoral study, the reading of other genres of literature for personal enjoyment also proves crucial for pastors. The occasional good novel or work of science fiction for the sole purpose of personal delight may offer a needed break for the pastor's mind.[50] The mind needs rest in order to think clearly and reading less dense material on occasion may result in a rested mind read to think more clearly in other studies. Even still, the learning process of any believer, especially pastors, can never come to a halt; it must be constant.

Pastors must be life-long learners because the life of a Christian is a life-long pursuit of knowledge from the God of all knowledge and truth. John Stott explains that G. Campbell Morgan, even as a man without a seminary degree, was in his study by 6 o'clock every morning.[51] A commitment to learning and study is necessary not because God requires long office hours or a certain word count in sermons, but because God expects excellence and thoroughness from the pastor who has devoted his life to the gospel ministry. Paul echoed this attitude by writing, "For I do not want to see you now just in passing. I hope to spend some time with you, if the Lord permits" (1 Cor. 16:7). Therefore, pastors should aim for thoroughness and their best work, especially in the study. MacArthur notes that Paul was aiming to do everything in his ministry as "sound and permanent, worthwhile and lasting."[52] However, for a pastor to commit himself to such an intellectual

---

49. Piper, *Brothers, We Are Not Professionals*, 107.
50. Lloyd-Jones, *Preaching and Preachers*, 193.
51. Stott, *Between Two Worlds*, 201.
52. MacArthur, *1 Corinthians*, 463.

Preparation and the Pastor's Personal Life

task, he must also allow his brain to rest and rejuvenate so he can be thorough and do his best work. For a pastor to do his best work, however, he must also take time to rest, relax, and revitalize. This comes in the form of the pastor's leisurely activities.

The Leisure Time of the Pastor

The pastor must aim to do his best work while he is serving the Lord in his respective ministry. However, if the pastor is working so much that he has no leisure time, he will experience ministerial burnout. Thus, the pastor must have time every single week to rest and rejuvenate. This comes through a day off, taking Sabbath, intentional rest, and results in longevity in the ministry.

The Pastor's Day Off

Rick Reed recalls hearing Lewis Sperry remark about Robert Murray M'Cheyne's life and writes, "No one can have a spiritual ministry without a physical body."[53] Hence, a large part of soul care is mainly caring for our bodies. While Paul did advocate that training oneself for godliness is of value in every way, he also mentioned the fact that physical training does have value (1 Tim. 4:8).

Thus, physical exercise is, in fact, a necessary element to physical health, but pastors must also take care to prioritize their day off. This day off gives their bodies time to re-energize for the week ahead. Pastors must understand that Sunday is not a day off; it is a workday. Therefore, a pastor must find another day to rejuvenate and recuperate and it comes by honoring Sabbath in his own life.

The Pastor's Sabbath

The pastor's Sabbath is not only a necessary element of every week, but it is also a biblically warranted practice. Mike Glenn

---

53. Reed, *The Heart of the Preacher*, 192.

once preached a sermon in Southeastern Seminary's chapel service called "The Marathon of Ministry." In this sermon on 1 Kings 19:1–8, he says, "You step away, and you sit down. You remember the Sun came up this morning and did not ask your permission, and it will go down in the evening and will not check with you on its way by. It does not depend on you, and that is good news! You need Sabbath to remember that."[54] Dr. Glenn gets it right: Sabbath is the only way we can remember the reality that it is God who is sovereign over every single detail going on in the world, including the pastor's life. If pastors are to neglect Sabbath, it will be a difficult task to shepherd his entrusted congregation in submissive reverence to Christ.

The Pastor's Rest

Jared Wilson gives great wisdom to pastors who walk into their office on Monday morning, tired and fatigued. He notes that while they may feel downtrodden and as if they do not amount to much, God is no less God now than he was before.[55] Pastors need to immerse themselves in the truth of Matthew 11:28: "Come to me, all who labor and are heavy laden, and I will give you rest." Jesus promises rest to those who have tirelessly worked all week for God's glory, and this group includes pastors on Mondays. Rest is a must for those who shepherd God's people.

The Result in Longevity

Thus, it follows that when pastors give special attention to their off day, their personal Sabbath, and finding rest in Jesus Christ, a lengthy ministry can be the result of such activities and priorities. Leroy Forlines offers some timely comments in his work, *Biblical Ethics*, by stating that leisure activities are necessary for the

---

54. Southeastern Seminary, "Mike Glenn—The Marathon of Ministry—1 Kings 19:1–8."

55. Wilson, *The Pastor's Justification*, 34.

Christian life (God created such activities), but they can become, if misused, means to sinful lifestyles.[56] Therefore, pastors must pay special attention to their leisure activities in order that they may glorify the Lord and not allow them to steer toward a way of neglecting the spiritual disciplines within their lives, which could result in shorter tenures.

Soul Care Results in Preparedness

In summary, pastors cannot truly prepare their hearts to preach if there are not at least four priorities in their lives. The devotional life is the absolute foremost necessity for pastors to lead a congregation to spiritual health. Apart from practices of spiritual discipline, a pastor has no foundation for leadership in the local church; however, pastors must also make prayer a particular focus of their lives. Not only is prayer to be a personal, private matter for pastors in their own Christian life, but it is also to be a prioritized attitude for their families and in the day-to-day responsibilities of the ministry.

However, another way in which pastors can look to be adequately prepared to preach is to work out his intellect through various means of study and knowledge. Pastors must have an internal goal of living a life of learning because this is the attitude of those who follow Christ. Disciples, according to Scripture, are lifelong learners, and pastors must model this type of spirituality for their congregations to emulate. Along with studying, however, is the problem of preaching their own sermons that stem from their study. If pastors neglect their intellect, the apparent result is the preaching of someone else's sermon in the pulpit. Therefore, pastors must give adequate measures of time to be studious for the edification of the congregation he is leading, and for the glory of the Lord Jesus.

Therefore, the pastor's leisure time cannot be ignored in their soul care. Leisure time allows pastors to rest, relax, and stand in

---

56. Forlines, *Biblical Ethics*, 195–96.

awe of the sovereignty of Creator God in their own lives. H.B. Charles notes that it will take time to nurture a congregation to spiritual health.[57] Thus, a long-term pastorate can be traced back to a daily renewal of the mind through an intimate union with the head of the Church, Jesus Christ.

---

57. Charles, *On Pastoring*, 57.

4

The Disciplines of Expository Preparation

Part 1

ALTHOUGH THE PRIMARY SPIRITUAL disciplines are biblically warranted practices, there are other disciplines pastors must typify to prepare to preach. Preparing oneself to preach is, most definitely, a spiritual priority. A pastor who is not prepared to preach will become spiritually in danger of lazy soul care. Thus, both spiritual and homiletical preparation is necessary for these two reasons.

First, both correlate with the pastor's soul. Jonathan Edwards expresses to his readers that human souls are active parts of a person, not passive. He summarizes one's soul as the *human itself*, not merely one part of the human.[1] Of course, this is not only demarcated in Edwards's writings but many other great theologians as well.[2] When a pastor prepares his soul for the task of preaching, he disciplines himself by the spiritual practices warranted from the Word of God. Nevertheless, when a pastor is pursuing the construction of his sermon through hermeneutical techniques, he

---

1. Smith, "Religious Affections," 201.
2. For further study on the soul as the full human being, see Sinclair Ferguson's *Devoted to God: Blueprints for Sanctification* and C.S. Lewis's *Mere Christianity*.

is also disciplining himself for godliness by using his skillset to prepare his sermon adequately.

Second, sermon preparation should be an outflow of the pastor's soul care. The spiritual life of the pastor (only succeeding the Word of God) is a primary element of the pastor's sermon preparation. Of course, this does not indicate that pastors must only preach their Bible reading plans each year, but the vitality of their spiritual life permeates the content of their sermons. Joel Beeke says preaching "often grows out of the preacher's own experience of Christ in the midst of his sorrows and sins."[3] Beeke indicates that the pastor's own life experiences are what fuel his preaching. Thus, a pastor's ministry is to be an overflow of his spirituality through his personal life. Therefore, this chapter will be an examination of the disciplines in the pastor's life regarding his sermon preparation.

The Disciplines of Expository Preparation

As pastors should focus on the spiritual nature of sermon preparation, they must also focus on the homiletical characteristics of sermon composition. Although these disciplines do not fall under the category of "spiritual disciplines," they are, however, disciplines which pastors must prioritize to prepare their sermons for the glory of God. This prioritization begins with submission to Christ.

Submission to Christ in the Preparation of Sermons

Because the pastor is first a believer, his vocational undertakings begin with his submission to Christ. In other words, what pastors devote themselves to is what will be manifested through their lifestyle and conduct. This is a foremost perspective for all pastors to understand; their values and beliefs dictate how they live and what they do.[4] Therefore, the pastor's submission to Christ must be of first importance because how pastors act are the results of what

---

3. Beeke, *Reformed Preaching*, 39.
4. Freeman, "The Spiritual Discipline in Personal Formation," 94.

they value, to whom (and to what) they are loyal, and what they believe. Thus, pastors must follow Jim Shaddix's recommendation and never lose God in the sermon preparation process.[5] Losing God in one's sermon preparation is the result of a lack of submission to Him.

For a pastor to begin his preparation faithfully and thoroughly, he must begin in submission to Jesus Christ. Jesus entreats all people, especially pastors, to come to him and find rest.[6] Submission to Christ is not *only* resulting from respect, reverence, awe, and worship, Submission to Christ also comes when we cast our cares at his feet to find our identity and rest in Him (Matt. 11:25). Rest also assures that pastors are reveling in Christ for their competency to the task of pastoral ministry. Charles Bridges explains that for ministers to be involved in such a spiritual task (pastoral ministry), they must possess spiritual character to administer such duties.[7]

Therefore, pastors must submit themselves entirely to Jesus Christ, the author and perfecter of their faith (Heb. 12:2). The pastor's faith is rooted and grounded in Jesus Christ through his submission to him. So, we must address the necessity of the pastor's spiritual life.

The pastor must base his spiritual life solely on his union with Christ. Therefore, the pastor must actualize his spiritual life in two ways. First, submission to Christ involves devotion. God's desire is for us to know him (Heb. 4:12). Therefore, it is not possible to know God if one is not devoted to God. Knowledge of God does not come from sporadic interaction with His Word, nor does it come from one's own experience or reason. Knowledge of God comes from one's absorption of God's Word.

Second, submission to Christ means forsaking all sinful activity in one's life. Human beings often define themselves by the world's criteria rather than by biblical principles. They no longer believe in an innate sinful nature within each person. In the words

---

5. Vines and Shaddix, *Power in the Pulpit*, 317.
6. Ferguson, *The Whole Christ*, 171.
7. Bridges, *The Christian Ministry*, 26.

of David Wells, "Americans . . . do not believe in original sin."[8] This belief could not be further from the truth. Instead, one finds that sinfulness is the problem that keeps all believers from submitting their entire selves to Christ (James 4:7). Therefore, when submission to God is a foremost priority, one finds a new perspective on life.[9] When submission to God is the essential facet of the pastor's life, nothing else is of any value, for God becomes all that he values. Thus, when God becomes all one values, the pastor's life marks itself by the overflow of such values.[10]

Hence, submission to Christ is the first and necessary step to disciplining oneself for expository preparation. Preparing one's soul to preach begins with Christ, but it also extends to actions resulting from one's devotion to the Lord himself.

Prayer in the Preparation of Sermons

The most critical element for the preparation of sermons is the pastor's commitment to prayer. Spurgeon notes that if a pastor prays with any other attitude other than an ordinary Christian, he is a hypocrite.[11] In fact, pastors are to pray as ordinary people, for that is who they are. The most elemental purpose of this ordinary type of prayer is to understand the necessity of utter dependence upon the Lord Jesus for pastors as they prepare and as they preach. Preaching, though done through human effort, is never done *only* by human effort, but by divine empowerment. Thus, pastors ought to outperform every person in their church through prayer.[12] Hence, prayer is not merely an act of mere devotion; it is "the Christian's vital breath and native air."[13]

---

8. Wells, *The Courage to Be Protestant*, 191.
9. McGrath, *Mere Discipleship*, 4.
10. Allen, *The Preacher's Catechism*, 36.
11. Spurgeon, *Lectures*, 42.
12. Sanders, *Spiritual Leadership*, 99.
13. Ibid.

The Disciplines of Expository Preparation: Part 1

Prayer is more than an act of mere devotion or spiritual habit; it is the most vital element of any believer's life, and especially the pastor's life. Prayer is petitionary, intercessory, communicative, and, most importantly, indispensable for all people who claim to be in communion with the Lord Jesus Christ. Therefore, as they prepare to preach, pastors must be people of prayer. The pastor must bathe his sermon in prayer. Spurgeon taught that the prayer closet is the best place for study because the Author of Scripture is the most profitable teacher, even better than those who comment on such truth.[14] In other words, pastors must not neglect prayer as they prepare their souls and sermons. Luther was busy and still prayed; so can we.[15]

If pastors, through their submission to Christ, are dependent upon Christ for their strength to preach, they will understand that the power of Christ living within them is the only means through which ministerial accomplishments are made manifest. Joel Beeke looks back in time to Thomas Boston, a Puritan theologian, who advises that if pastors want to follow Jesus' example to be fishers of men, they must first follow his example of much prayer.[16] Thus, pastors must be on their knees in prayer long before they engage in the duties of pastoral ministry. This is the attitude of Jesus and must also be the attitude of all pastors.

Therefore, prayer is more than mere communication between you and God. It is "a relationship which cultivates an awareness of the presence of the Heavenly Father."[17]

Nevertheless, an awareness of the presence of God during prayer should lead the pastor to devote himself to the Lord through profoundly thinking about the truths of God Word.

---

14. Spurgeon, *Lectures*, 43.
15. Sanders, *Spiritual Leadership*, 100.
16. Beeke, *Reformed Preaching*, 81.
17. Freeman, "The Spiritual Disciplines in Personal Formation," 96.

Scriptural Meditation in the Preparation of Sermons

Scriptural meditation is another discipline that must manifest itself in the life of the pastor and his sermon preparation. Meditation on Scripture allows the pastor to think about the truths of Scripture and apply them to the way in which he lives. The application of biblical truth affects the way one pastors. Charles Bridges states, "It is important also to cultivate this habit in the bent of our own work—that is, that a Preacher should think as a Preacher—marking everything (like any other man of business) with the eyes of his own profession."[18] To "think like a preacher," as Bridges would suggest, is to consider what biblical meditation is and then to apply these types of habits to your life.

The definition of biblical meditation comes best from the prophecy of Jeremiah: "Your words were found, and I ate them, and your words became to me a joy and the delight of my heart" (Jer. 15:16). This eating is metaphorical of someone consuming physical nourishment.[19] Calvin writes that biblical meditation in the life of a believer is what yields the best and sweetest fruit spiritually.[20] Here are two considerations to yield the best fruit regarding biblical meditation.

First, meditation is necessary for sermon preparation because it prompts the pastor to indulge his mind and heart in the Word of God. Meditation begins with the pastor's pursuit of Christ through submission to Christ and prayer, but it also extends to the pastor's consumption of the Word of God. A desire for the Word is necessary for pastoral ministry (1 Tim. 4:13), but it is also necessary for the preparation of sermons. This necessity exemplifies itself when pastors "know nothing more among [us] except Jesus Christ and him crucified" (1 Cor. 2:2). In other words, the content of our preaching is to be founded upon Christ Jesus and his crucifixion. Robert Picirilli notes that this is the only topic worthy

---

18. Bridges, *The Christian Ministry*, 209.
19. Swanson, *Dictionary of Biblical Languages)*.
20. Calvin, *Institutes*, 128.

of emphasis in Paul's preaching, and must be the case in every pastor's preparation.[21]

Hence, pastors only know and emphasize Christ and him crucified by engrossing themselves in the Word of God; then the Word of God also challenges and shapes their minds to think biblically.[22] Therefore, pastors must actively be pursuing knowledge of the truth that can only be found in God's Word, for it is the foundation of their ministry.

Second, after immersing oneself in the Word, a pastor must internalize the truth discovered. Biblical meditation is not achieved unless the truths considered are internalized and lived out. In summarizing the spirituality of Leroy Forlines,[23] Barry Raper notes that little familiarity with truth does not sanctify one's life, but "truth must be understood by the mind, embraced by the heart, and obeyed in life."[24] In other words, the way biblical truth applies to the heart of a person through the means of meditation. Meditation leads to an internalized faith that characterizes itself through the life of an individual. Therefore, John Stott recommends that pastors must probe the text like a bee with spring blossom, a hummingbird and nectar, a dog with a bone, and a cow chewing his cud.[25]

Therefore, meditation is more than merely reading and re-reading a text. Instead, it is the internalization of the Word of God in the life and ministry of the pastor so that when he preaches Christ, lives can be changed by divine power. This internalization, however, cannot be undertaken unless the pastor has a specific time and method for Bible intake.

---

21. Picirilli, "1,2 Corinthians," 28.

22. McGrath, *Mere Discipleship*, 10.

23. Forlines has much to say regarding the spirituality of one's life through the mind, heart, and will—what he calls the "Total Personality." To further review Forlines's theological approach to spirituality, see Forlines' chapter on Sanctification in *The Quest for Truth*.

24. Raper, "Sanctification and Spirituality," 112.

25. Stott, *Between Two Worlds*, 220.

Expository Preparation

Bible Intake in the Preparation of Sermons

The pastor must be consciously aware of his Bible intake, for it is the source in which he will attain godliness. The Bible instructs all, including pastors, to spend time in God's word. For instance, Hosea explains the importance of knowing God and spending time in his Word when he says he desires "the knowledge of God rather than burnt offerings" (Hos. 6:6). Burnt offerings, in the Old Testament, were heartless sacrifices from the children of Israel in place of faithful obedience.[26] God delights in his children faithfully obeying him rather than them offering up burnt offering-like actions out of mere obligation. Likewise, the psalmist echoes such an idea in Psalm 147: "the Lord takes pleasure in those who fear him, in those who hope in his steadfast love" (Ps. 147:11). Those who truly fear God will obey him out of reverence and awe and will seek to know Him rather than merely what is commanded in Scripture. Thus, pastors must look unto the Lord for godliness and growth that one achieves through faithful obedience in spending time in God's word.

The pastor's Bible intake, in specific regard to his sermon preparation, plays an intricate role as well. Jim Shaddix and Jerry Vines proffer that preaching is not a sermonic option, but a sacred obligation, because God has spoken through his Word. Therefore, we must preserve the spoken word of God that is contained in our Bibles, so pastors might proclaim it correctly to those who listen.[27] Thus, without the foundation of Holy Scripture, pastors have no basis for proclaiming the Lord Jesus to their congregants correctly. Hence, a consistent Bible intake is necessary.

The only content worth sharing in a sermon is the Word of God. It is sufficient to change hearts because it is God's authoritative Word that is inerrant and infallible. Thus, the preacher must impregnate his sermon with the content of the Word of God because the Word alone is powerful to save sinners (Rom. 1:16–17). Unless the sermon is full of the Word of God, it is not a sermon

---

26. Reed, "Hosea," 55–56.
27. Vines and Shaddix, *Power in the Pulpit*, 60.

The Disciplines of Expository Preparation: Part 1

at all. Spurgeon posits that if pastors would give their people the complete, raw truth of the Scriptures, their fruit will soon be actualized because pastors are faithfully shepherding the flock of which they have been entrusted.[28]

As we have shown, the spiritual disciplines are necessary, but they are also required for sermon construction and preparation. However, much more is required of the pastor in order to construct a sermon faithfully that will yield fruit, and this task begins with the pastor's sanctification.

---

28. Spurgeon, *Lectures*, 78.

5

The Disciplines of Expository Preparation
Part 2

IN THE PREVIOUS CHAPTER, the first portion of the disciplines of expository preparation primarily focused on the personal nature of soul care. In this chapter, the disciplines become a bit more generalized and outward focused rather than inward and specific. Now that the soul of the pastor is cared for, let's take a look at some habits once he enters his office—let's continue!

Sanctification in the Preparation of Sermons

Pastors must be moving toward holiness through the process of progressive sanctification. Joel Beeke describes such importance when he says, "The holiness of a minister's heart is not merely an ideal; it is absolutely necessary for his work to be effective. Holiness of life must be his consuming passion."[1] This process is similar to how Paul instructed the Corinthian believers to "Be infants in evil, but in your thinking be mature" (1 Cor. 14:20). Maturity is the goal of the Christian life. Sinclair Ferguson relates the situation in which the Corinthians found themselves to babies on Christmas

---

1. Beeke, *Reformed Preaching*, 67.

Day playing with wrapping paper rather than the gift they had received.[2] They are completely enamored with the wrong thing. In other words, if pastors are ignoring the sanctifying grace of God in their life, it will not be present in their sermons. Thus, this lack of presence will then translate to their congregation. When there is no personal sanctification in the pastor, it will result in a lack of sanctifying activities in the lives of congregants.

Therefore, the sanctification of the pastor is an indispensable activity because the pastor sets the example to his congregation. The spiritual disciplines allow the pastor to pursue godliness while progressively becoming more and more like Christ himself, all while emulating for the congregation what true spirituality looks like in everyday life. While the disciplines are the foundation that sanctifies the pastor through the Word. The result will be evident in his sermons. When this goal of Christlikeness is the priority, the sanctification process will always be primary.[3] Here are two reasons why this process should take primacy in the pastor's life.

First, this earthly journey is a pilgrimage preparing us for the life to come. Jesus told his disciples that the only way to get to the Father was by Him (John 14:6). The term "pilgrimage" is a necessary term to comprehend because it conveys the idea that the Christian life is a marathon, not a sprint. Eugene Peterson remarks that Christian maturity is never realized in life by immediate action and results but over long periods through the processes of life.[4]

Second, sanctification is the lifelong pursuit of holiness. This lifelong pursuit of holiness is more than merely *trying* or *aiming* to be holy. Forlines notes that this process speaks of as a relationship between a person and God rather than a conduct of mere morality.[5] In other words, holiness does not come from merely being a *moral* person.

---

2. Ferguson, *Maturity*, 12.

3. Sinclair Ferguson. *Devoted to God: Blueprints for Sanctification* (Edinburgh, NSW: Banner of Truth, 2016), 7.

4. Peterson, *Long Obedience*, 17.

5. Forlines, *Quest*, 222.

Thus, for pastors to experience the sanctifying work of Christ in their life, they must devote their entire selves (mind, heart, and will) to Christ and allow His Spirit to guide their lives as they live and lead the church of God. Pastors must integrate their growth in holiness into their sermon preparation because it is vital to emulate for their congregants what it means to live the Christian life. Congregations need to hear (and see!) that the Christian life is achievable, and pastors must be the embodiment of such truth. Bridges notes, "Just as He delivered us from the overall reign of sin, so He has made ample provision for us to win the daily skirmishes against sin."[6] In other words, Christ gives us victory and pastors must be the personification of the victory believers are promised through Jesus Christ.

To become sanctified, one must learn the truth by the Word of God (through Bible intake, prayer, and meditation) and must practice it through his actions. Forlines' total personality provides the most logical conclusion for such statements: truth must be "understood by the mind, experienced and felt in the heart, and acted upon by the will."[7] It is through these means and to this end that pastors must devote themselves as they grow in the grace and likeness of our Lord Jesus Christ.

This growth not only manifests itself through actions and attitudes of the pastor's personal life, but the pastor will also actualize them in his sermons. Therefore, the sanctification of the pastor plays a primary role for the sermon preparation each week in his life because these first five disciplines—submission to Christ, prayer, meditation, Bible intake, and sanctification—supply the power needed to complete the next four disciplines dealing intricately with sermon preparation, beginning with biblical interpretation.

---

6. Bridges, *The Pursuit of Holiness*, 71.
7. Forlines, *Quest*, 239.

The Disciplines of Expository Preparation: Part 2

Interpretation in the Preparation of Sermons

Some scholars claim that proper interpretation draws out the meaning of a passage and correctly personifies it,[8] while others claim that in order to do correct exegesis, the pastor must read the passage to understand the original meaning contained within.[9] In other words, biblical interpretation ensues when the pastor proclaims to his people what the original author meant for his original readers.[10] Correct exegesis is necessary because without it, the pastor will proclaim a message out of line with biblical teaching. It is as Robert Thomas says, "if the explanation of what the author meant is missing, so is the heart of Bible exposition."[11] Thus, to correctly exegete a passage of Scripture, a pastor must discipline himself to understand the meaning and themes of a passage so he can accurately convey and proclaim them to his congregation.

Understanding the meaning of a particular text is not an easy task. However, it is most necessary for the proclamation of the Word of God because it serves as spiritual direction for those who hear it.[12] Therefore, exegesis, before the construction of a sermon, is necessary because the Bible "does not lie open before us. It does not simply appear as God's word but as God's word in human word."[13] Though the Bible is, in fact, the Word of God, it is also the words of human authors—it is considered a theanthropic book.[14] Robert Plummer writes, "Note, Luke does not say, 'I prayed, and the Holy Spirit brought to my mind the stories of Jesus to write.' Luke was a historian—engaged in real historical research. Nevertheless, as an inspired companion of the apostles, Luke was also

---

8. Shaddix and Vines, *Power in the Pulpit*, 181.

9. Robinson, *Biblical Preaching*, 66.

10. York and Decker, *Preaching with Bold Assurance*, 19. (hereafter, *Bold Assurance*)

11. Thomas, "Exegesis and Expository Preaching," 181.

12. Winner, "Preaching as a Spiritual Discipline," 520.

13. Meuer, "What is Biblical Preaching," 183.

14. Geisler, "Introduction and Bible," 253.

God's revelatory agent."[15] Because the Bible is a book of divine revelation through the words of men, the truths contained within it must be meditated upon and diligently interpreted so the pastor might achieve correct interpretation.

Biblical interpretation is the most difficult and most time-consuming effort of sermon preparation.[16] In the words of Martyn Lloyd-Jones, pastors must aim to be honest with the text. He notes that directly approaching a biblical text to pick out an idea in which interests them would be dishonestly approaching the Bible.[17] He observes that analyzing and philosophizing a text is "utterly to abuse the Word of God."[18] Thus, to interpret the Bible correctly, the pastor must diligently discipline himself to study the Word, he must understand the magnitude of preparing sermons, and he must always consider the weight of communicating divine truth as spiritual direction to one's congregation.

Nevertheless, interpretation is just one meager step in the preparation of sermons. Once biblical interpretation has occurred, many other pieces of the sermon must be placed into the material used for construction. One specific piece which cannot be ignored is theological instruction as a part of one's proclamation of the Word of God.

Theological Instruction in the Preparation of Sermons

Preaching is a message from God; therefore, it is theology. Since theology is always present in preaching, it is "God talk."[19] Peter exhorts his readers to always be ready to give a defense for the hope that is in them (1 Peter 3:15), and this requires a foundation of doctrinal certainty. In other words, Peter encourages those to whom he writes to defend the gospel to which they have devoted

15. Plummer., *40 Questions About Interpreting the Bible*, 33.
16. Zuck, *Basic Bible Interpretation*, 10.
17. Lloyd-Jones, *Preaching and Preachers*, 212.
18. Ibid., 214.
19. Smith, "Theology, Preaching, and Pastoral Ministry," 340.

themselves. It is from this word "defense" (*apologia*) where our English word "apologetics" comes.[20] Therefore, a defense of the gospel necessitates theological knowledge. If pastors are to correctly interpret and understand the doctrinal truth of which is contained within the biblical text, the only result when one preaches is "theology coming through a man who is one fire."[21]

Lloyd-Jones states that the chief end of preaching is to give people a sense of God and his presence.[22] Since God and his presence are understood and experienced through His Son, Jesus Christ, preaching must be Christological. For preaching to be Christological, it must be centered upon and solely focused on Christ. This was the message the reformers proclaimed: *Solus Christus*. Joel Beeke affirms that if one loses any sense of Christ in their preaching, the substantial tenant of Christianity is forsaken.[23]

Such theological instruction in preaching requires an attitude of devotion to God and his Word, focusing upon learning all truth contained within Holy Scripture. It is similar to Packer's method of theologizing which involves developing one's theological framework from the Scriptures rather than from another scholar's work.[24] Therefore, theological knowledge does not only come from Bible colleges or seminaries, though such formal education is beneficial to those who can obtain it. Instead, theological knowledge should begin with one's study of the Bible. Hence, this knowledge that comes from one's study of the Bible should translate into every facet of one's preaching. Tom Nettles offers a similar approach in his principles for preachers: 1) preaching should propagate doctrine, and 2) preaching is the product of doctrine.[25]

In other words, Nettles is suggesting that preaching is doctrinal from its beginning. Doctrine and theology fuel the sermon

---

20. Liddell et al., *A Greek-English Lexicon*, 208.
21. Lloyd-Jones, *Preaching and Preachers*, 110.
22. Ibid.
23. Beeke, *Reformed Preaching*, 402.
24. McGrath, *Mere Discipleship*, 113.
25. Nettles, *The Privilege, Promise, Power, and Peril of Doctrinal Preaching*, 5–6.

and fill it with content. Thus, an absence of doctrine is no sermon worth preaching. The propagation of doctrine is the beginning of the pastor's efforts to develop and construct a sermon. However, the development of doctrine in the exegetical stage of preparation does not fizzle out as the process moves forward; instead, it stays the course throughout until the pastor closes his Bible on Sunday evening. Thus, the necessity of theological instruction is to instruct a congregation in the knowledge and truth of God.

Pastors do their congregation a disservice when there is an absence of theological instruction in their preaching. Many pastors spend their time looking into cultural trends and fads that they believe aid in their preaching. However, they neglect the notion that God's Word is sufficient to fill the content for their sermon. Yet, many congregants do not understand the weight of theology, so they ignore it altogether. They ignore the reality that knowledge of anything at all is knowledge of God.[26] Consequently, what many Christians do not understand is that the very nature of Christian truth is theological. This reality does not imply that preaching ought to be incomprehensible. Instead, it aims to strengthen its content with biblical truth rather than stories or material from popular culture. The Bible is sufficient to fend for itself; therefore, pastors must allow the text in which they preach to do as much. They must, as Spurgeon says, "give a clear testimony to all the doctrines which constitute or lie around the gospel."[27]

The centrality of the gospel in theological instruction must be the goal of every pastor as he proclaims the message of God in Christ each week. However, the reality one must realize is that theological instruction is gibberish without application.

---

26. Frame, *The Doctrine of the Knowledge of God*, 128.
27. Spurgeon, *Lectures*, 74.

The Disciplines of Expository Preparation: Part 2

Application in the Preparation of Sermons

If a pastor's sermon lacks application, his sermon is void of the characteristics necessary for Christian proclamation.[28] Expository preaching in general is absent unless there is application of exposed truth to the hearers. York explains, "Our job is more than just explaining the text. Our job is to make it vibrant, fresh, and accessible."[29] Application is accomplished best by having a central idea in which to communicate the entire sermon in one short sentence. Some scholars call this a central theme,[30] while others name it the big idea.[31] Regardless of one's terminology, the sermon should have one main *proposition* explaining how the passage of Scripture relates to the listener.

An important exhortation to aid pastors in applying their sermons is to preach from their hearts to the hearts of their hearers.[32] The application of the biblical text should affect the pastor before it ever applies to those under his proclamation. The pastor's heart must be like the psalmist who declares, "Search me, O God, and know my heart! Try me and know my thoughts! And see if there be any grievous way in me, and lead me in the way everlasting" (Ps. 139:23–24)! Only truth that applies to the heart of the pastor will more readily apply to the listener.[33] The Puritan preachers embodied this principle in the most substantial ways. They were conscious of every single effort to reach the heart of their congregation by the format of which they proclaim the gospel.[34] Thus, the goal of preaching is so the Word of God will be at work in the pastor, which will translate to the working of God in the hearts of the congregation (1 Thess. 2:13). However, for the pastor to apply

---

28. Pace, *Preaching by the Book*, 50.
29. York and Decker, *Bold Assurance*, 7.
30. Ibid., 139.
31. Robinson, *Biblical Preaching*, 31–48.
32. Vines and Shaddix, *Power in the Pulpit*, 320.
33. Pace, *Preaching by the Book*, 51.
34. For a wonderful and clear presentation of the Puritans and their application of Scripture, see Beeke, *Reformed Preaching*, 369–84.

biblical truth correctly to his hearers, he must be present in their lives and be able to observe how his congregants live.

Observing Life in the Preparation of Sermons

Observing life is a phrase claiming that pastoral leadership comes best by characterizing relational ministry with his congregation.[35] When pastors are shepherds, they understand the necessity of spending time with their sheep. Shepherding is never successful if there is no time spent with the sheep of which they are in charge. Therefore, pastors must spend time with those under their leadership and care.

Unless the pastor is spending adequate time with his people, he will have difficulty applying his sermons to those sitting in the pew. This type of preaching is what the Puritans of old call *experiential preaching*.[36] Capill offers the same advice to his readers with a probing question: "If we can't connect the dots between biblical truth and life as it really is, what makes us think our people will after the sermon?"[37] Thus, the observation of life is necessary to apply the sermon carefully to those under his watch and care.

Sermon Preparation Sparked by Soul Care

The disciplines for expository preparation are necessary for the pastor's soul care, but they are also necessary to aid in the pastor's construction of his sermon.

Though this list of disciplines is not exhaustive, it does prompt pastors to step back and take an honest look at their sermon preparation. Submitting himself to Christ through prayer, meditation, and Bible intake will allow the pastor to begin his sermon preparation

---

35. Capill, *The Heart is the Target*, 81–96.
36. For a definition of experiential preaching, see Beeke, *Reformed Preaching*, 23–42.
37. Capill, *The Heart is the Target*, 90.

The Disciplines of Expository Preparation: Part 2

with a clear mind and a pure heart because it will focus on growth in holiness that is only aided by the Spirit of God.

However, once the spirituality of the pastor is in full view, his sanctification is the focal point of his spiritual life. The sanctification of the pastor is necessary for the pastor to embody the faithful yet fruitful Christian life. This, then, will allow the pastor to interpret the Bible with pure motives and without sinful presuppositions as he exegetes the text he will be preaching. Yet, the pastor must not only search for the meaning of the text, but also the theological underpinnings detailed within. Only then can the pastor apply the sermon to his listeners. By building relationships with his congregants, he can determine the most appropriate ways to communicate the text from his heart to the heart of his listeners because he has observed life with them.

6

Preparation as Worship

AUGUSTINE EXPLAINS HOW MEANING can sometimes be dependent upon the person when he writes, "What is time? If nobody asks me, I know; but if someone asks me, I don't know." You see, when God acts, he acts through his spoken Word. This is how God created the world (Gen. 1) and how he gave us Scripture (2 Tim. 3:16). Thus, words and meaning are important for establishing the divine authority of the Bible.

The Bible as Authority

Paul conveys, "All Scripture is breathed out by God" (2 Tim. 3:16), which means God's word is a crucial element to understanding the divine nature of Scripture and its inspiration. Scripture is a product of the very breathe of God; it is divinely given to humanity.[1] Words and meaning do have distinct characteristics, but they also do have a close relationship with each other for learning and communication.[2] Because preaching is a communicative act and

---

1. Ibid., 43.
2. Forlines, *Quest*, 49.

deals with how the congregants can learn the Scriptures, its words must be translated and interpreted carefully and correctly. If biblical interpretation is done ineffectively, the congregation's learning ability can be disparaged. Therefore, the pastor must pay close attention to the way in which he prepares sermons because if biblical truth is incorrectly conveyed, it will limit the application of truth to the hearers.

The Bible and its authority are the most important elements for preaching because anything otherwise is not preaching according to biblical standards. Therefore, we must not be timid in our proclamation of such truth, and one should proclaim these truths with authority because those who preach stand in the stead of Christ as they speak. In a sermon on biblical infallibility, Spurgeon says, "Modesty is a virtue, but hesitancy when we are speaking for the Lord is a great fault."[3] This is advice that all pastors must heed when they stand behind the sacred desk. Biblical authority is emulated through the act of preaching and all pastors must understand the weight of such a task in worship. However, the element of preaching in worship does not begin when a pastor opens his Bible on Sunday morning getting ready to preach. Instead, it begins in his office while he prepares and constructs his sermon.

Worship Commences from the Pastor's Study

While worship is the aim of preaching, the Holy Scriptures is the essence of biblical preaching; therefore, all that that Bible sets out to do is what preaching will accomplish.[4] The Scriptures testify to the authority of God's Word when one preaches them faithfully and correctly. However, the preparation for preaching begins much earlier than when the pastor stands in the pulpit on Sunday as he must prepare himself through soul care and spirituality. He must also prepare and construct his sermon according to biblical standards of expository preaching. Furthermore, all of these steps

---

3. Spurgeon, "The Infallibility of Scripture."
4. Piper, *Expository Exultation*, 160.

are acts of worship to God made manifest through the pastor's personal life. Thus, a pastor must take explicit and intentional action to prepare sermons, while regarding all that is done as worship to the Lord.

A Reformed View of Preaching

Preaching cannot be seen as a weekly task to be taken lightly but it must be approached with much caution and humility. However, in many evangelical pulpits, preaching has lost its importance. Unfortunately, many churches focus more on music and the "culture" of the church rather than aiming to be guided by the Word of God in all areas of life (which would include such things as culture and music). Nonetheless, preaching is where all of this begins, for it is the proclamation of God's Word, and God's Word is what governs the doctrine and practice of the local church. Thus, preaching must aim for the following elements.

First, preaching must aim to communicate the knowledge of God regarding salvation. The Bible repeatedly speaks of salvation as the "knowledge" of God (Is. 33:6; Jer. 3:15; Luke 1:77; Rom. 2:20; 1 Cor. 12:8; 2 Cor. 4:6; Eph. 4:13; 1 Tim. 2:4; Titus 1:1). Therefore, it is necessary that those who are under the instruction and proclamation of the Word of God to not only hear, but to understand what is being proclaimed. Otherwise, salvation is not possible because knowledge of God involves *understanding*. It is the task of preaching that affords a pastor the opportunity to convey the truth of the Bible as understandable so those hearing the proclamation can be understood and understanding will lead to salvation.[5] Nothing ascribes worship to God more than the saving of those who are lost (Luke 15:10).

Second, preaching must implore the congregation to think biblically with the desire of worshipping God. Once salvation has occurred, the purpose of preaching is to entreat the congregation to think biblically about the way in which they live. Genuine

---

5. Lloyd-Jones, *Preaching and Preachers*, 39–40.

Preparation as Worship

spirituality that is born out of love for God expands to all of life. Thus, to think biblically is to immerse oneself in the Word of God so much that it affects the way he lives his life. This is not only the calling of pastors but the calling of all Christians.[6]

Therefore, Christians must think biblically—this is a must! In a world of constant relativity and indigenous disgust for Christianity, it is essential for Christians to make God the center of life rather than themselves.[7] In other words, living and thinking biblically is living with Christ and his cross at the center of our lives.[8] This, of course, does not imply that life will be prosperous with large bank accounts or massive amounts of property. Instead, it infers that the lives of believers, who are faithful and committed to Christ, will be lives of leisure and freedom because the believer is honoring God's pursuit of him through Jesus Christ.

Third, preaching must invoke theologizing. Theologizing, essentially, is the act of doing theology for oneself. All believers are not called to glean their doctrine from others who have done the work for them. Paul says believers should "work out [their] own salvation with fear and trembling" (Phil. 2:12). McGrath shows the importance of theology: "Pelagianism is the natural heresy of zealous Christians who are not interested in theology."[9] Those who are not interested in theology (pastors included!) must understand that Christianity is a religion of the heart, will, and *mind*. Therefore, the Christian mind is necessary for the pastor standing in the pulpit each week and for his hearers. Theologizing, especially in preaching, is to instruct the congregation to apply the deep truths of Scripture to all of life for the glory of God.[10]

---

6. Beeke, *Reformed Preaching*, 71.

7. David Wells does a wonderful job explaining the necessity of what it means to think biblically in a world that is post-Christian. To study the problem of postmodern thought, see The *Courage to Be Protestant: Truth-lovers, Marketers, and Emergents in the Postmodern World.*

8. Peterson, *Long Obedience*, 57.

9. McGrath, *Mere Discipleship*, 112.

10. Beeke, *Reformed Preaching*, 70.

Expository Preparation

Each of these steps for pastors do not come without hard work. It takes rigorous activity and devotion to develop and deliver Christ-centered, God-honoring, and Spirit-filled messages that glorify God and edify the believer. For this reason, the pastor must take time out of his week to develop and deliver his sermons.

A Plea to Study

Since preaching is the focal point of every worship service, preparing for each service accordingly must be a vital element of the pastor's weekly activities. Though the pastor coming under the Word of God is a necessity for faithful preaching, there is a distinct difference between a pastor's personal life as a believer and his task as a pastor of a local congregated body. Hence, the pastor must engage in the spiritual disciplines through personal activity in the Word, but how does this aspect of instruction and conviction bleed into the construction of sermons?

Every pastor must aim to be a biblical theologian—that is, they must aim to discover how each text they preach fits into the grand narrative of Scripture.[11] The task of biblical theology seeks to make sense of the entire Bible as one comprehensive story, which entails exegeting specific passages in light of the story of Scripture.[12] Therefore, as the pastor aims to interpret the biblical text, he must also continue to keep forefront the story of redemption as Scripture unfolds for him through a specific passage. Interpretation through the process of exegesis is rigorous, and it takes time to think through the difficulties of biblical truth. There are times when the Bible does not make sense to the human mind. Thus, the pastor must work through these issues to exhort his congregation to salvation, thinking biblically, and to do their own theology.

If the truths one preaches never first apply to the one preaching, it will be difficult to effectively apply the same truths to those who are listening. Therefore, a rigorous study schedule is of the

---

11. Piper, *Brothers, We Are Not Professionals*, 92.
12. "The Place of Biblical Theology", 200.

Preparation as Worship

utmost priority. Pastors must study to perform faithful exegesis. Pastors must study to settle the confusion between biblical passages. Pastors must study to apply the truth in Scripture to themselves first. Pastors must study to see how Scripture can mold them into the person of Jesus Christ. Pastors must study to exhort those in the congregation to such a standard of living that is conveyed from God's authoritative and infallible Word. The purpose of studying is to show how even the pastor's life when he is not at church is an act of worship to God. Therefore, the pastor must emulate this worshipful attitude and persona within the study each week.

A Plea to Preach Your Own Sermons

Because the purpose of studying is such a personal act of worship, the way in which one prepares and constructs a sermon is important for pastoral study. The importance of preaching your own sermons and not copying from another is a direct result of one's belief about the preeminence of preaching as worship to God.[13] The simple fact that a pastor would preach someone else's sermon to the congregation shows the uncertainty of calling within their own life. Otherwise, they would preach and aim to do it with faithfulness and courage, and, most importantly, through their own words. This act, however, is often an intentional act from pastors.[14] One author declares, "There can be no accidental plagiarism any more than there can be accidental bank robbery!"[15]

One specific way in which pastors tend to overlook the necessity of preaching one's sermons is a lack of applying the biblical truths of their sermons to themselves first. Ignoring such an act is

---

13. For a short but fruitful discourse regarding preaching your own sermons, see Scott M. Gibson. *Should We Use Someone Else's Sermon?: Preaching in a Cut-and-Paste World*.

14. I would be amiss to claim that every pastor does such a thing intentionally, for young ministers with no experience may have not been taught proper ways to construct a sermon. However, most pastors who commit such an act, I believe, are ones who do so intentionally because our age in immediacy has brought about laziness in the processes of study and sermon preparation.

15. Corn, "A Few Borrowed Words About Plagiarism."

Expository Preparation

the final stroke before a pastor resorts to someone else's material. The Puritans expressed such importance in application.[16] Pastors must return to such practice of prioritizing self-examination! The days are evil, Paul says in Ephesians 5:16, so we should "make the best use of [our] time." Making the best use of our time does not allow for pre-written sermons from other pastors because of misguided priorities (that is, prioritizing other things over study and self-examination). It is a disloyal, unfaithful injustice to the Lord Jesus when pastors make excuses to avoid sermon construction and preparation.[17]

Yet, the most important aspect to this plea is understanding the limit placed on worship when one is preparing to preach. True biblical worship is not brought about by pious actions and behavior. Instead, biblical worship is brought about through the heart.[18] Worship involves the affections and so must our preaching. As it was defined in chapter 3, this is the essence of experiential preaching that was emulated by the Puritan preachers. The pastor must align his own affections to the biblical warrants of which he will proclaim, then implore those under his preaching to do the same with their affections, as well.[19]

As pastors approach the task of preaching, they must prepare for this task by understanding the worshipful nature of sermon construction and sermon delivery.

Sermon Preparation and Delivery as Worship

Since preaching is an act of worship, the pastor stepping up to the sacred desk to preach must be reverent and serious, because preaching hangs eternity in the balance for all who hear.[20] The task of preaching alone brings its own difficulties to overcome.

---

16. Gibson, *Should We Preach Someone Else's Sermon?*, 65.

17. To read on about excuses preachers makesee Gibson, *Should We Preach Someone Else's Sermon?*, 61–63.

18. Piper, *Brothers, We Are Not Professionals*, 257.

19. Ferguson, "Preaching as Worship," 99.

20. Lloyd-Jones, *Preaching and Preachers*, 99.

Preparation as Worship

However, another task of the pastor is to be the worship leader for each service because the Word of God directs our worship. Thus, if the pastor tries to make worship an effect rather than a lifestyle of glory and honor to God, he loses the centrality of the Word of God in worship. It could possibly cause the pastor to lose biblical centrality in his preaching and preparation. Thus, here are four reasons why the pastor can never lose the Bible as his central component to preaching in worship.

The Gospel is Good News

Paul David Tripp explains that one of the most crucial elements to understanding the gospel is understanding that the gospel is for all people when he writes, "No one gives grace better than a person who is deeply persuaded that he needs it himself and is being given it in Christ."[21] Hence, the pastor preparing himself to preach by allowing himself to come under the authority of the text will then give the best presentation of the gospel because he has first had his affections transformed by the Lord Jesus Christ himself. The gospel has several components to its makeup, and they are the following.

First, man is fallen and without Christ. It is not secret that mankind is in a predicament spiritually.[22] This predicament comes from the fall in Genesis 3 where Adam and Eve disobeyed the commands of God and placed their fleshly priorities above God's standard of living. This disobedience thereby affected all their posterity (Rom. 3:23) and has left each human being in a state of sinfulness separated from God.

Second, in the person of Jesus Christ, God came down to humanity to save them from their sins. Jesus Christ, the Son of God who is truly God and truly man, came to earth, lived a perfect life, and died the death for human beings in their place, which does two things that manifest themselves in the next two components.

---

21. Tripp, *Dangerous Calling*, 122.
22. Forlines, *Quest*, 187.

Third, those who believe in Christ are justified. Justification by faith alone is the doctrine upon which Christianity stands or falls. If justification is denied or ignored, Christianity is demarcated to mere moralism. Mankind is innately sinful and the only remedy for such sinfulness is a perfectly divine being who can pay humanity's debt in their place. Because humanity is sinful, they cannot make their way toward God in any fashion (John 6:44). Yet, because God is holy, he must judge all sinfulness. However, God in his kindness sent his Son to pay the penalty for human beings so they can know him. In other words, Jesus Christ's death justifies sinful humanity before God (2 Cor. 5:21).

Fourth, those who are justified are so because of substitutionary atonement. Substitutionary atonement is the only viable belief for a follower of Jesus Christ; it is the only biblical option to satisfy the wrath of God for the sins of humankind. This component of the gospel is also an important factor to note because it understands the death of Christ to be a literal death for sin, not a mere example of God's hatred of sin. Instead, the wrath of God due human beings was poured out on Christ through his death on the cross in order that humanity might gain access to the Father through Him.

The gospel is good news because it has nothing to do with human beings, but only is possible by the work of God in the lives of human beings through His Spirit. This gospel is the only message worth proclaiming, and pastors must get it right as they preach.

Preaching is Proclamation

In the grand scheme of preaching, a vitally important aspect is proclamation. To proclaim the message of the gospel is the evangelize. "'Proclaim' is complementary to the more specific term 'evangelize' (*euangelizomai*) or the phrase 'announce the good news,' which contains within its meaning the object that is announced or proclaimed—the good news."[23] Since the purpose of all Christian life is to be witness for the Lord Jesus (Acts 1:8), the pastor

---

23. Farrell, "Preach, Proclaim," 626.

witnesses to the Lord through Christian proclamation. Though there is a difference between preaching and evangelism[24], the two cannot be separated in the life of the pastor. The pastor must be adamant to never lose the priority of his own personal evangelism because of his life in Christ as a believer himself. However, the proclamation to those under his preaching every week must be a bit different.

Preaching, unlike evangelism, is geared toward believers (for the most part). The purpose of preaching is to proclaim the gospel to those gathered as the body of Christ. Therefore, most (if not all) of the audience of which the pastor is preaching will be believers. Hence, there is a necessity for the gospel to shape how one lives. However, if unbelievers are present—which is a likely possibility—pastors must always aim to preach Christ crucified and risen for our salvation.[25]

Salvation is brought about by proclamation (Romans 10:17). Preaching is the proclamation of the good news of Jesus Christ to those gathered as a body of believers (1 Cor. 2:13). Both methods of proclamation ascribe the Lord glory because they are both warranted practices of Scripture. But most importantly, preaching is worship because it exults God as the sovereign Being who does everything for his own glory and our good.

Preaching is Exultation

The goal of all things done in the church is the glory of God. Even creation itself ascribes to this purpose. The psalmist exclaims, "The heavens declare the glory of God, and the sky above proclaims his handiwork" (Ps. 19:1). Piper gets it right in declaring that God delights in all he does. He writes, "If God is not under constraint by forces outside himself to act contrary to his good pleasure, but rather acts only out of the overflow of the joy of his boundless

---

24. For further study on the gospel and evangelism in the life of a believer, see Mark Dever's *The Gospel and Personal Evangelism* and J.I. Packer's *Evangelism and the Sovereignty of God*.

25. Keller, *Preaching: Communicating Faith in an Age of Skepticism*, 14.

self-sufficiency, then all his acts are the expression of joy and he has pleasure in all that he does."[26] Piper's comments on God taking pleasure in all he does helps his readers understand the magnitude of God delighting in himself in all of his glory. Therefore, preaching is done for God's glory because it is God's Word in which God delights. This is the heart of exultation—understanding the purpose of corporate worship as the "visible, unified knowing, treasuring, and showing of the supreme worth and beauty of God."[27]

In summary, worship is the goal of all that is done within the local church and within the lives of believers. Our lives, according to the apostle Paul, are living sacrifices to God as our act of worship (Rom. 12:1–2). However, to truly understand what it means to worship, one must begin with the Scriptures. It is the Bible itself that is the foundation of the truth that is communicated. The Bible is true because it is God's revealed Word to humanity, but also because it coheres with reality; it is rational. To worship God in Spirit and truth is to worship him as the Creator and Sustainer of all things. This also will fill the sermon's content, which alone is worship to God because it is a regurgitation of his Word to his people, so they will live for his glory in worship to him.

However, for a pastor to truly understand and lead a worship service, this process must begin in his own heart. The worship leader (that is, the pastor) should be immersed in the Bible to apply to himself first, then he can effectively apply it to his hearers. The application spans itself into many different areas to include the way he studies, why he studies, and the sermons he preaches. Then, once the pastor understands the weight of preparation, he can then proclaim the good news of the gospel in a worship service for the glory of God.

---

26. Piper, *The Pleasures of God*, 51.
27. Piper, *Expository Exultation*, 71.

7

Basis for Worship

WORSHIP OF THE TRIUNE God is the essence of life as a believer in Jesus Christ. Worship in the believer's life means that he is to align his volition with the prescribed method of worship in Scripture.[1] The lifestyle of a believer manifests one's worship of God as the worth of God is evidenced. Therefore, Christian worship is more than mere singing or being involved in a local church; it is a lifestyle of manifesting the glorious work of grace by the triune God in one's life.[2] The transformation that takes place in a person's life at regeneration begins the life of devotion and commitment to God. Yet, this devotion to God is not forced upon a believer, but it is a natural outflowing of his union with Jesus Christ.[3]

---

1. Calvin, *Institutes*, 63

2. For a more detailed description of worship, see Timothy M. Pierce's *Enthroned on Our Praise: An Old Testament Theology of Worship*. Though Pierce defines worship exclusively from the Old Testament, there is much New Testament application within his work. He uses Old Testament law and tradition to sustain New Testament worship through the fulfillment of promise through the person and work of Jesus Christ. He describes worship as an "ascription of worth" alongside a "relationship between creation and Creator."

3. Peterson, *Long Obedience*, 50.

Expository Preparation

However, a sizable portion of Christian worship comes in one's commitment to a local church. Provided within one's commitment to the local church is a weekly proclamation of the gospel through the preaching of the Word of God. This notion, of course, commences an important aspect to introduce this chapter: that we should never isolate preaching from worship. Preaching is an element of worship; it works in coherence with singing, prayer, liturgy, confessions, and ordinances.[4] Yoder explains the importance of preaching when he describes it as the "public address form of ministry in which a word from God intersects with a human need."[5] Thus, as the sermon expounds on God's message to his people, preaching must be maintained as the focal point of a worship service.[6]

Therefore, this chapter will demonstrate how preaching is the primary activity in worship by examining the truthfulness and authority of the Scriptures, by describing a posture of worship through the pastor's study, and by describing the act of preaching as worship through glory to God, proclamation, instruction, and exultation.

Worship begins with the Scriptures

Though the Bible is not the only means for the revelation of God's self to humanity,[7] it is, however, the primary means through which God reveals his justifying, saving grace to a fallen world.[8] "Faith comes by hearing," Paul writes, "and hearing by the *Word of God*" (Romans 10:17, emphasis mine). Preaching allows all who sit

---

4. Piper, *Expository Exultation*, 16.

5. Yoder, "The Sermon as Fulcrum: The Role of Preaching in Worship," 37.

6. Ibid., 39.

7. For further study on this topic, see John M. Frame's *The Doctrine of the Word of God*.

8. For a more detailed take on God's self-revelation through Scripture, see Forlines's chapter on revelation in *The Quest for Truth*, or Part 2 of John M. Frame's *The Doctrine of the Word of God*.

under its proclamation to consider the truths declared. So, then, how we comprehend this truth is extremely important.

Truth is the condition upon whether biblical interpretation succeeds or fails, because biblical interpretation is the direct explanation of the Word of God, the source of all truth.[9] This proposition brings to light the notion that truth only comes to the seeker when he correctly interprets the truth revealed from God. Jesus asks the Father to "sanctify them in the truth; your word is truth" (John 17:17). If this proposition is accurate, then one must examine how it relates to biblical worship that is only brought to fruition through the discovery of truth.

The Bible as Foundation of Truth

Because truth is the assembling of facts as they are experienced through reality,[10] a pastor must understand the rationality and realistic nature of the Bible itself. The ultimate test of truthfulness of Scripture is its coherence with reality. So, regarding the Bible, one must seek to justify the Bible as truth rather than fairy tales or fiction. Therefore, one does this in two different ways: affirming God as the ultimate truth-Giver and proposing the Bible as God's revealed Word.

The existence of God must be rationally interpreted through the lens of how truth is realized. It is not enough to simply "prove" God's existence through a certain *apologetic argument*, though these means can be sufficient to "prove" God's existence. Instead, a more fully orbed approach to ascertain the existence of God is through rationalizing the knowledge of truth; he is the sovereign truth-Giver. The penultimate method for discovering truth is by properly understanding which particulars cohere the most with reality.

The Bible as God's revealed Word must be the starting point for the pastor who is to preach in worship. The Triune God has revealed himself to us by communicating within himself to

---

9. Vanhoozer, "Lost in Interpretation? Truth, Scripture, and Hermeneutics," 89.

10. Nash, *Life's Ultimate Questions*, 228.

humanity. The Father speaks to the Son, the Son speaks to the Father, and both to the Spirit and the Spirit to both.[11] Peter declares that "men spoke from God as they were carried along by the Holy Spirit" (2 Peter 1:21), so the process of the Bible being understood as God's Word begins with God revealing himself to the apostles by his Spirit, then succeeds to how the apostles witnessed the full revelation of God himself in the person of Jesus Christ.

In essence, God is a communicator; therefore, God has communicated to humanity by his Word through his relationship with humanity, and through Jesus Christ, the Godman.[12] Therefore, God's truth is reality.[13] Since the Bible is God's revealed Word to humanity, it must be of utmost priority to the one who will prepare to preach. The essence of preaching is the proclamation of God's revealed Word to a gathered assembly of believers. Therefore, the Bible must be the foundation of all that is done in a worship service, from the singing to the preaching.

The Bible as Basis of Content

Because the Bible is the foundation of all things true, it must serve as the content for all sermons. The Bible is the supreme source for content in the sermon because the Bible is the source of life for a believer. It is described as "profitable," in 2 Timothy 3:16. Paul is reminding Timothy that "the basis of its profitableness lies in its inspired character.[14] If a pastor has a spiritual foundation (built upon the disciplines of expository preparation), then the Bible will be prevalent throughout his sermon's content. The truth of the Bible resonates with the pastor because his delight is in the Word of God and this brings about clarity throughout the sermon construction process. This clarity for the pastor is a result of a healthy regimen of expository preaching in his weekly habits.

---

11. Frame, *The Doctrine of the Word of God*, 42.
12. Forlines, *Quest*, 46.
13. Piper, *Expository Exultation*, 161.
14. Guthrie, "*Pastoral Epistles: An Introduction and Commentary*," 182.

Basis for Worship

Jason K. Allen explains how this process was beneficial personally in his spiritual development. He recalls that during his early days of ministry this weekly preaching was the most influential element to his growth.[15] Thus, a pastor will fill his sermon with the Bible in three distinct ways.

First, the Bible must be the source of all knowledge and content in the pastor's sermon. There is no sermon apart from the Bible. So, for a preacher to preach effectively and for his preaching to serve as worship to God, he must approach the Bible, study the Bible, write the Bible (through notes), think on the Bible, pray through the Bible, and then preach the Bible. If a pastor is to ascribe all glory to God during his sermon, he must understand the nature of preaching as declaring Christ to a gathered congregation for the one purpose glorifying God.[16] Thus, the pastor should impregnate his sermons with the Word of God rather than aiming to quote well-known scholars or try to use excellent rhetoric to persuade the congregation to action. God blesses faithfulness that labors with the text to declare its correct meaning and interpretation. Therefore, the pastor must leave the content to the Bible and the conviction to the Spirit, for this is their roles as divine aids in preaching.[17]

Second, the pastor must fill his sermon with knowledge from his Bible study. As a pastor studies his Bible personally, sermonically, and intellectually, he must read the Bible with the end goal of worship. While Piper is correct when he says the ultimate aim of all Bible reading is the "the worship of God's worth and beauty," we should also say that this is the goal of preaching as well.[18] Therefore, as a pastor aims to worship God in his preaching, he must mold the content of his Bible study into the manuscript that will become his sermon week after week with the goal of acknowledging God's

---

15. Allen, *Letters to My Students*, 35.
16. Beeke, *Reformed Preaching*, 62.
17. Meuer, "What Is Biblical Preaching?", 187.
18. Piper, *Reading the Bible Supernaturally*, 62. Though Piper's aim throughout this work is geared toward reading the Bible for its worth in the life of a believer, it is not difficult to see how this concept also relates to the preaching of the Word of God.

worth and beauty. Therefore, the pastor must allocate time in his week to allow the content of his study of Scripture to be molded into the sermon itself.

Third, the Bible contains language that must be studied and communicated. The Bible is the penultimate way in which God has provided sinful humanity a way to know him. Calvin proffers that the Bible is God's expression of love and grace toward God's elect to bring them nearer to him.[19] However, the Bible was not written by infallible authors, so their language is not precise, for they were human beings moved by the Spirit of God.[20] Since the authors of Scripture were normal human beings, their language is sometimes vague and difficult to interpret. Therefore, as the pastor desires to worship God in his preaching, he must endeavor to study the language of the Scriptures so he can communicate the truth of God effectively and correctly.

Nevertheless, the pastor cannot truly communicate such a book with "language barriers" unless he believes in the authoritative nature of the Bible. Therefore, the Bible as authoritative is necessary for true biblical worship because it is the governing force behind all worship elements.[21] This is the foremost principle within the Regulative Principle: The Bible governs all activities during a gathering of believers in worship to God.

---

19. Calvin, *Institutes*, 26.

20. Frame, *The Doctrine of the Knowledge of God*, 216.

21. For a more detailed study of the "Regulative Principle," see Ligon Duncan's "Traditional Evangelical Worship."

8

Why Expository Preparation?

WHY IS EXPOSITORY PREPARATION truly necessary? It is because the Bible is our sole authority for doctrine and practice. When we draw from the Bible our doctrine, it informs our practice of proclaiming the gospel of Jesus Christ as His messengers. We do this, of course, through the disciplines of expository preparation. These disciplines are how one grows into a state of maturity in holiness, and pastors must ascribe themselves to these disciplines. Peter expressed the necessity for spiritual growth when he commanded those under his leadership to "grow in the grace and knowledge of our Lord and Savior Jesus Christ" (2 Peter 3:18); Likewise, Paul instructed Timothy to "be strengthened by the grace that is in Christ Jesus" (2 Tim. 2:1). These commands indicate that their readers are to be in continuous growth and strengthening in the knowledge and grace that comes from Jesus Christ. Such strengthening and growth for the believer comes from the spiritual disciplines, and the pastor who sees the disciplines as important will see growth in his spirituality.

Pastoral Growth by Discipline

As the pastor's growth ultimately is contingent upon his participation in the spiritual disciplines, he must be habitually involved in the disciplines of Bible intake, prayer, meditation, service, and evangelism.[1] Though the disciplines are the foundation upon all the pastor's ministry, it is primarily the foundation upon which pastors can preach faithfully the Word of God. Faithful biblical preaching flows from the pastor's soul and reaches the hearts of those to whom he is preaching. Since the disciplines prepare the pastor's heart to engage exegetically and homiletically with the Word of God when the pastor neglects the spiritual disciplines, his sermon preparation becomes lacking.

For this reason, the disciplines should be primary in the pastor's life, because the disciplines are how pastors are to grow in holiness. Growth in holiness is a biblically warranted necessity for all who profess their loyalty to Jesus Christ, so this includes the pastor as his life as a believer. However, it also includes the pastor's different activities in which he pursues to prepare his sermons. Thus, the spiritual disciplines necessitate the pastor to address his own soul before he ever constructs a sermon.[2]

The pastor cares for his soul in four specific areas: his devotional life, prayer life, study habits, and leisure time. The pastor's devotional life is necessary, because in it the pastor immerses himself in the Word of God. Like every other believer, the pastor must engage his mind and heart with the biblical text through intake, prayer, and meditation. Each of these methods of devotion to God are for the purpose of knowing (mind) the Word and internalizing (heart) the Word. Furthermore, the knowledge of God through the Word and the internalization of such truths in the Word are what

---

1. For a full list of the spiritual disciplines, see Donald S. Whitney, *Spiritual Disciplines for the Christian Life*. In this resource, Dr. Whitney outlines, in several chapters, the disciplines and their importance in the lives of believers.

2. For an excellent article on preparing the pastors heart to preach, see R. Kent Hughes, "The Preacher's Toolkit: How Do I Prepare My Heart to Preach?" *The Gospel Coalition*, accessed December 17, 2019, https://www.thegospelcoalition.org/article/preachers-toolkit-how-do-i-prepare-my-heart-to-preach/.

Why Expository Preparation?

affect the wills of all believers, especially those who lead God's church through the pastoral office.

Nonetheless, the disciplines are not the only avenue through which pastors should prepare their soul to preach. A pastor's study habits, and leisure time are a necessity throughout the weekly tasks of pastoral ministry. Studying for sermons entails more than simply thumbing through the biblical text and/or a few commentaries. Studying for sermons takes time so the pastor can determine the meaning of certain discourses in Scripture while also aiming to apply the propositions of these passages to those who will hear them proclaimed. Applying pericopes to a specific congregation takes devotion and diligence in the study. Studying is also necessary for the construction of one's own sermons. If a pastor is to preach at all, he must aim to preach his own sermons which result from his personal devotion to Jesus Christ.

So, for a pastor to correctly prepare his own heart to preach, he must do so by the disciplines of expository preparation. The first way in which the pastor disciplines himself to prepare his own heart to preach is by his own submission to Christ. Right belief always informs right living, and this method of living is the foundation upon which all growth in holiness builds itself. The way to holy living is through one's commitment to the Lord Jesus himself, which entails a relationship with him.

The second way pastors discipline their hearts is through prayer. Prayer is the dependence upon the Lord Jesus Christ for the power to live the Christian life. However, it is also the dependence upon the Lord Jesus for the power to prepare sermons through the power of the Spirit. These first two disciplines are the bedrock of all other disciplines. However, they are also the underpinning of the pastor's sermon preparation as he disciplines his heart to preach.

A third discipline for pastors to prepare his heart to preach is through the act of biblical meditation. Biblical meditation is the internalization of biblical truths to morph one's life into the image of Jesus Christ. Meditation assists a pastor to think like one and to form habits of spiritual maturity to grow in the Christian life. Fourth, the discipline of Bible intake allows the pastor to meditate on such dialogue from Scripture. Without a consistent intake of God's Word, the pastor has no message to proclaim to a congregation. Therefore, a consistent intake of God's Word entrusts the pastor with a consistent message of truth each week.

A fifth discipline in the preparation of sermons is the pastor's own sanctification. A pastor's becoming like Christ must be his foremost activity for his lifetime. It is the pastor who will be the model of godliness for those under his leadership. The pulpit is one way in which the pastor can emulate a sanctified lifestyle to those in his congregation. Thus, the discipline of sanctification is modeled through the pastor's preaching. Therefore, a sixth discipline for expository preparation is biblical interpretation. Biblical interpretation is not simple task, but it is a necessary one, nonetheless. It is through biblical interpretation that true application can be extrapolated. Therefore, it must be done with integrity and precision. A seventh discipline is the theological instruction for pastors as they prepare to preach. Preaching is theological and therefore, it compels the pastor to become a theologian. Preaching communicates the truths of God through the intense study and interpretation. However, it does not require a formal degree, but a devotion to the Lord Jesus Christ. Then can the eighth discipline of application be formed by the pastor. Yes, biblical interpretation and theological instruction are, in fact, necessary for a sermon.

However, a sermon is not complete without application. Unless the listeners are hearing how theology and biblical truth can change their hearts toward Christ Jesus, there is no sermon. However, application can only come to fruition through a ninth discipline of observing life with one's congregation. Observing life is Murray Capill's term for building relationships with one's congregation. Thus, the pastor can only know the situations of those in his congregation if her is to spend time with them building relationships. These disciplines allow the pastor the opportunity to sit in his office and consider the weight of preparing a sermon that is biblically centered and worshipful to the Lord. Though biblical teaching is good, teaching is informational. Preaching, however, should be transformational. It must transform the heart of the pastor, and as the pastor preaches those same truths will transform the hearts of those who hear.

The Necessity of Expository Preparation

Therefore, the spiritual disciplines do matter to the pastor for not only his own soul, but also for his heart as he prepares to preach. It is the application of the disciplines that will navigate the pastor toward holiness in order that his sermon preparation is done with integrity and devotion rather than out of obligation. Thus, expository preparation focuses on the preacher because all holiness, godly living, soul care, sermon construction, and sermon delivery begin with the pastor and his heart. If the pastor is focusing on his own heart during preparation, the sermon will come from a heart submitted to God and devoted to proclaiming Christ and him crucified. However, if there is not expository preparation, there can be no expository preaching. Therefore, the pastor must endeavor to prepare his own heart to preach so he can preach Christ. Expository preparation manifests itself in this mission—preparing a pastor's heart to preach for the glory of God.

May all who preach love the God whom they proclaim.

Soli Deo Gloria.

Appendix 1

"The Role of Spirituality for Sermon Preparation and Delivery"

Delivered at The 2020 Theological Symposium for The Commission for Theological Integrity of the National Association of Free Will Baptists

In their work, *Power in the Pulpit*, Jim Shaddix and Jerry Vines proffer, "Both who the preacher is and what he believes play vital roles in both sermon preparation and delivery."[1] The pastor's spiritual life will determine the effectiveness of his sermon preparation and delivery. Since the pastor's spiritual life is the determining factor for biblical vitality in the pulpit, the pastor must pay attention, then, to his union with Christ. The pastor must have a sturdy foothold on his personal life if he is to sufficiently prepare himself to preach. Only taking care of a sermon construction does not suffice as taking care of one's soul since one cultivates maturity through the inner self.[2]

---

1. Vines and Shaddix, *Power in the Pulpit*, , 95;102.
2. Gibson, "The Preacher's Personal World," 54.

Appendix 1

Therefore, to focus on his soul's maturity, a pastor must scrupulously examine his spiritual health and union with the Lord Jesus all the days of his life. Pastors must understand that to mature as shepherds in the Church of the Lord Jesus, they must love the God of whom they preach. It is a consistent fight throughout the pastor's sanctification, so the pastor's aim for excellence in the preparation and delivery of his sermons begins with his devotion to the Lord through the means of the spiritual disciplines. The spiritual disciplines establish the heart posture of the pastor through the medium of the spiritual disciplines, all for effective sermon delivery.

The pastor's participation in the spiritual disciplines, then, is the necessary element needed for correct exegesis. Though correct exegesis is possible without a heart posture steered toward God, the application for such a passage will be absent without personal preparation and soul care. Hence, a lack of preparation stems from the emphases within a pastor's ministry in the local church. This need for pastors to reorder their priorities has been noted in the analysis from LifeWay Research which conveys that overworked pastors tend to prioritize their pastoral duties over their spiritual growth and vitality.[3]

The reordering of a pastor's priorities, then, must begin with the foundation of his ministry: his union with Jesus Christ. If a pastor is to make his priorities in line with Scripture, then the pastor's first and foremost concern will be the care of his soul. Nothing is doable in Christian ministry without the power and strength of the Spirit within the pastor, especially that of sermon preparation and delivery. Therefore, soul care is the most necessary priority every single day of the pastor's life—it is his lifeblood. So, when a pastor focuses his priorities *first* on his soul, things such as sermon preparation and sermon delivery become achievable ends. Pastoral ministry and the task of preaching is worthy because the God

---

3. According to LifeWay Research, 39% of evangelical pastors spend less than four hours per week in personal devotion to the Lord apart from their weekly teaching and preaching duties. See, "Pastor's Long Work Hours Come at the Expense of People, Ministry."

who is working in and through the pastor does so to affect the hearers under the pastor's preaching.

The pastor must aim to attain union with the God of which he preaches in his sermons, but pastors cannot love God unless they pursue Him through a union with His Son. Therefore, this essay will present the primacy of the pastor's spiritual life—through the lens of the pastoral epistles—and demonstrate how it affects his sermon preparation and delivery.

The Pastor's Aim for Godliness

The spiritual disciplines play a vital role in the pastor's preparation because they allow the pastor to pursue holiness personally before stepping into the study or the pulpit to herald the good news of Christ. The fruit of the pastor's efforts to discipline himself for godliness will most likely be unseen in his lifetime but instead will be rewarded in eternity for his faithfulness. This was Paul's wish for Timothy and it should be the pastor's also: to "keep the faith" (2 Tim. 4:7) as he disciplines himself to lead a congregation to spiritual vitality through communion with Jesus Christ, our Lord. When viewed through the lens of gospel growth, the pursuit of godliness is a worthy goal for the pastor.

The Reason for a Worthy Goal

The goal of godliness is notable for all pastors to pursue because preaching is much more than just hard work; it's heart work.[4] The process of heart work is much more than simply one's relationship with Christ. Heart work is also demonstrated as one's confidence in his ability to communicate divine truth as a result of his union with Jesus Christ.[5] This is Paul's admonition to Timothy and Titus regarding the qualification of those who oversee the church of Jesus Christ—the overseer must be "able to teach" (1 Tim. 3:2) and

---

4. Reed, *The Heart of the Pastor*, xvi.
5. Lloyd-Jones, *Preaching and Preachers*, 122.

Appendix 1

"able to give instruction in sound doctrine" (Titus 1:9). If a pastor is to adequately and *biblically* shepherd the congregation entrusted to him, he must feed them the Word of God. It is the Word of God that nourishes the souls of the sheep, and, therefore, must be taught by one who is equipped to teach it.[6]

Paul shows Timothy that the preaching of the Word of God is a spiritual battle for the one proclaiming God's revealed word. In 1 Timothy 1, he reminds Timothy of the sufficiency of Jesus' coming to earth so that He might "save sinners of whom [he is] the foremost" (1 Tim. 1:15). Paul's emphasis on his struggles with sin is not to portray a false humility, but, instead, is used to "refer to God's patience and kindness waiting for people to repent."[7] This discourse, indeed, is conveyed to Timothy in such a way that he would have the same type of patience as the Lord did with Paul, because some are making "shipwreck of their faith" (1 Tim. 1:19). In other words, Paul shows Timothy here the importance of godliness and its priority in one's life as the mooring that ensures "a safe voyage to the harbor, the final haven of rest."[8] Paul's exhortation to Timothy is that his first pastoral goal was the pursuit of godliness. Yet, Timothy's second goal of pastoral ministry ought to be a concern for the sheep under his care—that is, their spiritual well-being. False gospels were infiltrating the church in every way, and Paul commands Timothy to expose them through his pursuit of godliness and the concern for his hearers' spiritual journey.

As Paul continues writing to Timothy, he proposes the idea that false teachers are prevalent in and around Ephesus. He writes that there is a modern-day apostatizing where "some will depart from the faith by devoting themselves to deceitful spirits and teachings of demons" (1 Tim. 4:1). It seems here that Paul not only warns Timothy of the possibility of one forfeiting his faith but also that there must be a sincere concern for the right preaching of the gospel. In verses 1–5 of 1 Timothy 4, we find Paul using the phrase

---

6. For a short treatment of this idea, see Lenski's, "Interpretation of Colossians, Thessalonians, Timothy, Titus, and Philemon," 584.

7. Köstenberger, "1–2 Timothy and Titus," 85.

8. Outlaw, "1 Timothy," 197.

"in later times" (or "in the last days," according to some translations). According to Köstenberger, this use of the term "last days" is directed toward the final apostasy before the second coming of Jesus Christ.[9] However, the "last days" or "later times" seem to indicate the period between Christ's resurrection and His second coming. According to Outlaw, there are continuous circles of departures from the faith in the "last days" of the church age.[10] Lenski concurs with Outlaw as well stating "ones had passed when Paul wrote, later ones would appear, and in one or the other or in more of them there would be apostasy."[11]

Paul's message to Timothy is that false gospels cause believers to deter from their faith, which may even lead to their apostasy. Therefore, Timothy must be diligent in his pursuit of an intimate union with Jesus Christ. Only the immersion of oneself in the Scripture can increase one's holiness. Thus, the pursuit of godliness is the only remedy for false teaching that will "save both yourself and your hearers" (1 Tim. 4:16). So, for the Word of God to affect the people of God by the power of the Spirit of God, the pastor must first be in union with Him through a personal pursuit of godliness; godliness must be his goal.

The Goal of Godliness

The only way in which pastors are set free is by treasuring themselves in the gospel of Jesus Christ.[12] To be set free by the gospel is to place one's entire dependence on it for spiritual vitality. There is only one avenue to spiritual vitality, and it is the gospel of Jesus Christ; anything else will lead to spiritual contamination and deterioration: "We will not grasp the truth, goodness, and beauty of God's Word apart from the Holy Spirit's work of conviction,

---

9. Köstenberger, "1–2 Timothy and Titus," 140.
10. Outlaw, "1 Timothy," 235.
11. Lenski, *Interpretation of Thessalonians, Timothy, Titus, and Philemon*, 618.
12. Wilson, *The Pastor's Justification*, 29.

illumination, and regeneration."[13] Therefore, for pastors to wholly achieve the end goal of godliness and holiness, Paul communicates doing two things: fleeing godlessness and pursuing righteousness.

Spurgeon notes, "For the herald of the gospel to be spiritually out of order in his proper person is, both to himself and to his work, a most serious calamity."[14] It is vitally important for the pastor to continually remind himself that a weighty portion of his pursuit of godliness means fleeing godlessness of any form. Paul writes, "But as for you, O man of God, flee these things" (1 Tim. 6:11). Paul uses verses 3–10 of 1 Timothy 6 to present many different vices which can enslave the young pastor, Timothy, in his pursuit of godliness. It is for this reason he commands Timothy to flee them. False teachers were ever prevalent in the vicinity of Timothy's church, so Paul instructs him to recognize these false teachers and their doctrine and *flee* them. The word flee is a very strong word which means to run away or shun, as if Paul is showing Timothy that his fleeing should a deliberate action rather than simply ignoring false teachers and doctrine.[15] Fleeing godlessness must be intentional by a shepherd feeding the flock. Lloyd-Jones proffers that being filled with the Spirit is not only character qualities but is the pursuit of godliness.[16] Thus, being a godly man involves pursuing righteousness and godliness.

Though Paul's first exhortation is to "flee these things," his continuation of this exhortation is to "Pursue righteousness, godliness, faith, love, steadfastness, gentleness" (1 Tim. 6:11). There are times when pastors are to flee from false teachings. Yet, there is always a command to pursue righteousness. Godliness cannot be obtained unless it is pursued. J.I. Packer notes that one of the most neglected priorities in the Christian faith currently is the pursuit of holiness.[17] This pursuit, then, is much more than mere behavioral

13. Kim, *Preaching the Whole Counsel of God*, 26.
14. Spurgeon, *Lectures to My Students*, 8.
15. Köstenberger, "1–2 Timothy and Titus," 192.
16. Lloyd-Jones, *Preaching and Preachers*, 122.
17. Packer, *Keep in Step with the Spirit*, 81.

modification, but a relationship with God himself.[18] John Piper encourages his readers to do the same by pursuing what he has called, Christian Hedonism. He writes, "We will not try to motivate their ministry by Kantian appeals to mere duty. We will tell them that delight in God *is* their highest duty."[19]

Paul exhorts Timothy with these same words. He encourages Timothy to "Fight the good fight. Take hold of the eternal life to which you were called and about which you made the good confession in the presence of many witnesses" (1 Tim. 6:12). Köstenberger offers a great argument regarding this truth: "Whether convenient or not, Timothy must preach the gospel (2 Tim. 4:2).[20] Paul's language in this discourse refers to the Greek athletic games and how there is a prize for those who compete and win. "What a prize there is to be won in this great contest for Christ!"[21]

Conclusively, Paul's exhortation to Timothy is commenced with the understanding that godly men, specifically godly pastors, "flee youthful passions and pursue righteousness" (2 Tim. 2:22). They do this so there may be some false teachers who might "come to their sense and escape from the snare of the devil" (2 Tim. 2:26). Of course, a pastor does not pursue righteousness through any other means but the spiritual disciples.[22]

The Importance of the Spiritual Disciplines

The spiritual disciplines are incredibly crucial for a pastor and, yet, sometimes merely hearing the word "discipline" can be defeating for him. Discipline, however, is a powerful word pastors must define and apply carefully for their spiritual good. The presence of the spiritual disciplines, or lack thereof, can either help or hurt a pastor.

---

18. Forlines. *Quest*, 222.
19. Piper, *Brothers, We are Not Professionals*, 67.
20. Köstenberger, "1–2 Timothy and Titus," 194.
21. Outlaw, "1 Timothy," 286.
22. Vines and Shaddix, *Power in the Pulpit*, 102.

Appendix 1

A study done by LifeWay Research records that one in seven pastors admit to Bible intake less than four times per week.[23] Although, many pastors make the claim to physically intake the Scriptures more than six times per week (almost 6 out of 10). The following are four reasons for local church pastors to discipline themselves for godliness.

First, pastors are believers. Pastors should not be placed on a pedestal because they are believers first and pastors second. They, like others, struggle in their own life. However, even amid struggles with life's difficulties, pastors should pursue holiness since whatever pastors are is what their churches will become.[24] If the pastor is a committed legalist, the church may become legalistic. If the pastor is a committed evangelist, the church will likely emulate him in his evangelism. Thus, if a pastor immerses himself in his Bible daily, the application of the Scriptures will naturally flow out of his speech, actions, and attitudes to affect the congregation in such a way that they would imitate his example (1 Cor. 11:1). Therefore, through their pursuit of Christ and godliness, the pastoral model of a devoted disciple of Jesus Christ is adamantly important. A pastor's devotion to Christ also affects how a pastor can *shepherd* his congregation by emulating how to be a devoted follower of Christ.

Second, pastors are shepherds. The Bible repeatedly refers to the church as a "flock".[25] So, it only follows that pastors are to shepherd those under their care and watch. Shepherding, then, means that the pastor is to focus primarily on his own spiritual life, but he must also be concerned with the spiritual life of those in his congregation. In other words, shepherding is soul care for those in one's congregation. Hughes explains, "There is no spiritual

---

23. While some would find this statistic somewhat admirable, I would argue that there is still much work to be done. Pastors are spiritual leaders, and there must be a consistent plan in place to be in step with the Spirit of God through communion with His Son. See, *Reasons for Attrition Among Pastors*, http://lifewayresearch.com/wp-content/uploads/2015/08/Reasons-for-Attrition-Among-Pastors-Quantitative-Report-Final1.pdf.

24. Wilson. *The Pastor's Justification*, 47.

25. Picirilli. *Teacher, Leader, Shepherd*, 81.

"The Role of Spirituality for Sermon Preparation and Delivery"

leadership apart from the fullness of the Holy Spirit. Therefore, it follows that if we aspire to pastoral leadership in the church, we must be full of the Holy Spirit."[26] The Holy Spirit is the only source through which pastors can shepherd their congregations to thriving in the Christian life. However, if one is to truly understand the nature of Christian discipleship (following Jesus Christ) and the nature of pursuing holiness, it will only come from the pastor's disciplined life of personally pursuing holiness. No one comes to possess a disciplined lifestyle by chance, nor does a church become healthier spiritually by the pastor desiring it upon them. It must be from an intentional investment and emulation of being spiritually disciplined in one's holiness pursuit.

Third, pastors are leaders. The author to the Hebrews wrote that his audience should "Remember your leaders, those who spoke to [them] the Word of God" (Heb. 13:7). Ultimately, then, a pastor will lead through his preaching. Although preaching is not the primary method to lead people because it is often less personable, it is a sufficient way for biblical truth to be spoken and heard. For some of the pastor's congregants, this may be the only time they will hear biblical truth. However, the writer of Hebrews also notes that leaders in the church are "keeping watch over [their] souls" (Heb. 13:17). Of course, then, to enact soul care within a local church is to do so through modeling a disciplined life.

Fourth, pastors are spiritual models. The pastor must prepare himself to be a Christian, to shepherd his flock, to lead his congregation, but he must also not neglect his preparation to model what a committed and devoted follower of Christ looks like in everyday life. Murray Capill explains that pastors should lead from a full reservoir and allow their members to see God's sovereignty over all areas of their lives, and for preachers to be suitable models of spirituality, they must understand that a Kingdom worldview is necessary to model such spirituality in the church.[27]

When pastors are full of the Holy Spirit, the church congregation will notice and want whatever he possesses. Paul wrote to

26. Hughes, *Disciplines of a Godly Man*, 186.
27. Capill, *The Heart is the Target*, 88.

Appendix 1

Timothy: "And what you have heard from me in the presence of many witnesses, entrust to faithful men who will be able to teach others also" (2 Timothy 2:2). Because God is a communicator, he ordains those shepherding his church to be relational in their efforts. Jesus told Peter to *feed His sheep* (John 21:17). The true task of pastoring comes in the form of leading the sheep to flourish in the Christian life, and the fundamental approach in which this commences is through sermon preparation.

The Necessity of Sermon Preparation

Because the pastor is first a believer, his vocational undertakings begin with his submission to Christ. In other words, that to which pastors devote themselves is what will be manifested through their lifestyle and conduct and ministry. This is a foremost perspective for all pastors to understand; their values and beliefs dictate how they live and what they do.[28] Therefore, the pastor's submission to Christ must be of first importance because how pastors act and live are the results of what they value, to whom (and to what) they are loyal, and what they believe. Thus, pastors must follow Jim Shaddix's recommendation and never lose God in the sermon preparation process.[29] Losing God in one's sermon preparation could be indicative of a lack of submission to Him. To prevent losing God in the preparation process, pastors must prioritize their godliness, seek God's approval of their life and ministry, and prepare to preach for God's glory and the Church's good.

The Priority of Godliness

Paul's words to Timothy regarding his pursuit of godliness and its importance are echoed earlier in his first letter. Paul not only commands Timothy to pursue righteousness but also commands him to train himself in the words of the faith (1 Tim. 4:6). In the

---

28. Freeman, "The Spiritual Discipline in Personal Formation," 94.
29. Vines and Shaddix, *Power in the Pulpit*, 317.

"The Role of Spirituality for Sermon Preparation and Delivery"

previous section of verses in chapter 4, Paul instructs Timothy to avoid false teachers but also instructs the church to do the same. However, verses 6–16 introduce Paul's commands to Timothy alone.[30] The main thrust of Paul's command here is nestled into verse 7: "train yourself for godliness" (1 Tim. 4:7). Simply put, "Godliness comes through discipline."[31]

The pastor's preparation deals with the heart, and when a pastor considers his task, he finds that his preparation is directly related to his spiritual life. To lead and preach for God's glory, the pastor must prepare his own heart; he must pursue holiness. This transformation does not happen because the pastor pursues holiness with adequate actions or with correct motives. Instead, it is given to him by grace that allows these activities to mold him into a godly being.[32] The pastor could *aim* for holiness, but it would not be reachable without the grace of God given to him by God's Spirit.

In other words, simply *wanting* to be holy or *wishing* holiness upon oneself does not characterize someone as holy. Donald Whitney helpfully clarifies that holiness is not attainable unless we pursue it.[33] Without sincere pastoral concern for self-character development, there is no spiritual formation or growth. Thus, a pastor's prioritized pursuit of godliness is necessary for three reasons.

First, the pastor's personal life depends upon it. Essentially, pastors cannot pursue holiness unless they are believers themselves.[34] Jesus teaches that only those who know him can pursue him (John 10:27). Therefore, no one person truly has a "spiritual" life until they are regenerated by the Holy Spirit. Nevertheless, the spiritual life of anyone (especially pastors) begins and ends with a rigorous pursuit of Christ himself.

This pursuit is necessary for those who profess Jesus Christ as their Savior because it demands they deny themselves, take up

---

30. Köstenberger, "1–2 Timothy and Titus," 145.

31. Whitney, *Spiritual Disciplines*, 10.

32. Emmert, "Resting in the Word of God: The Forgotten Spiritual Discipline," 37.

33. Whitney, *Spiritual Disciplines*, 2.

34. Pink, *Spiritual Growth*, 14.

Appendix 1

their cross, and follow him (Luke 9:23). So, a pursuit of holiness encompasses one's entire life. However, the task of a pastor can often be weightier because God also entrusts a congregation under his care and leadership (James 3:1); that brings spiritual demands to such a task. Therefore, the pastor's soul care should be a top priority for himself and his hearers (1 Tim. 4:16). Otherwise, ministerial repercussions may arise.

Second, the pastor's impact in the church depends upon his spiritual growth. A pastor's spiritual growth directly affects his influence within the local congregation he is leading. A pastor's influence comes from many different factors, but ultimately it pertains to his dealings with the congregation under his care and the application of his sermons. Yet, a pastor who knows not his people cannot adequately model spiritual growth. In other words, pastors are to model a life of godliness by pursuing Christ. Modeling spirituality can only happen if a pastor is pursuing Christ himself. Murray Capill explains that pastors who are spiritually malnourished will often "be like a blockage in a pipe preventing water from flowing freely."[35]

Third, the pastor's sermon preparation depends upon it. Ultimately, the pastor cannot adequately prepare to preach unless he is spiritually healthy. Spiritual health lies at the core of Christianity, so being spiritually healthy means that one is in constant relation with the spiritual disciplines prescribed in Scripture. If a pastor neglects to devote adequate time into the care of his soul, he can be guilty of "neglecting the gift of God that is in [him]" (1 Tim. 4:14).[36] Jerry Bridges summarizes that living for the Lord is the essence of what it means to be a disciple of Jesus.[37]

The pastor's discipleship—his following of Jesus—should be his soul's foremost priority. Otherwise, preaching should not be an option for him. Paul writes to Titus that elders (pastors) should "hold firm to the trustworthy word as taught, so that he may be able to give instruction in sound doctrine and also to rebuke those

---

35. Capill, *The Heart is the Target*, 82.
36. Bridges, *The Christian Ministry*, 194.
37. Bridges, *The Discipline of Grace*, 25.

who contradict it" (Titus 1:9). Therefore, if a pastor is spiritually unhealthy, he is unfit to guide a congregated body of believers to spiritual health (2 Tim. 4:2). Since spiritually unhealthy preaching is an oxymoron, it follows that a pastor must care for his soul to prepare his own heart to preach. Otherwise, there is a deficiency in the preparation of the sermon.

The Approval of God

Paul has more to say regarding Timothy's preparation to preach the gospel in his second letter. He writes, "Remind them of these things, and charge them before God" (2 Tim. 2:14). Ultimately, the goal of godliness is not for the pastor's confidence, but instead is for the approval of God himself. Godliness leads to holiness, and holiness is a necessary element to sermon preparation. It is one's holiness that leads him to do nothing more or less than *preach the text*. As Paul prompts Timothy, the pastor is to continually remind those under his care of the realities of God in Christ. The purpose of this repetitious prompting is so that Timothy's hearers will be continually reminded of the truths of the gospel which has been entrusted to them. Mohler emphasizes that leaders who lead well always show up with the same message, conviction, and principle.[38]

While Mohler's comments deal more with the leadership aspect of ministry, there is a direct correlation to 2 Timothy 2:14—pastors ought to remind their congregations of the glories of God in the gospel of Jesus Christ. The way pastors ought to do this is by "[Doing their] best to present [themselves] to God as one approved, a worker who has no need to be ashamed, rightly handling the word of truth" (2 Tim. 2:15). Here, Paul shows Timothy that the way to be *approved by God* is to avoid laziness and complacency in handling God's Word in the gathering of His people: "Timothy and all ministers will be evaluated concerning their handling of God's Word."[39] In other words, the approval of God is based upon how

---

38. Mohler, *The Conviction to Lead*, 95.
39. Outlaw, "2 Timothy," 327.

Appendix 1

the pastor handles His Word in the pulpit. So, then, preparation is necessary for pastoral ministry that is approved by God.

The Necessity of Preparation

There is a specific reason why sermon preparation is necessary for the life and ministry of a pastor, and it comes to us from Paul's letter to Titus: "For there are many who are insubordinate, empty talkers and deceivers, especially of the circumcision part. *They must be silenced*, since they are upsetting whole families by teaching for shameful gain what they ought not to teach" (Titus 1:10–11, emphasis mine).

Sermon preparation is necessary because just as there is a correct way to handle the text, there is also an incorrect way to handle the text. Lloyd-Jones posits, "You have got to be honest with your text. I mean by that, that you do not go to a text just to pick out an idea which interests you and then deal with that idea yourself. That is to be dishonest with a text."[40] If we are to "Declare these things," and "exhort and rebuke with all authority" (Titus 2:15), we must read and interpret the Scripture for what it is, not what we want it to be.

Therefore, preparing the sermon by first prioritizing the pastor's godliness and seeking the approval of God through his character and his handling of His Word is necessary because there are false teachers and false doctrine which are prevalent surrounding the church, and pastors are called to "teach what accords with sound doctrine" (Titus 2:1).

The Spiritual Nature of Sermon Delivery

Because sermon preparation is more than just an academic exercise, sermon delivery must also possess a spiritual nature within itself. Sermon delivery cannot be mere rhetoric from a pulpit but,

---

40. Lloyd-Jones, *Preaching and Preachers*, 212.

instead, must be viewed as communicating the pastor's heartbeat.[41] Preaching the heartbeat of the pastor can only be accomplished, however, if one's heart is in tune with the heart of God. Adam Dooley notes, "Before we animate our personality with the text, we must first align our lives to the text."[42] The goal of delivering the sermon, then, will be that repentance is the reaction of the hearers because of the charge to preach the Word.

The Goal of Repentance

The only true goal of preaching should be to declare the divine revelation of God Himself so that it might bring those under its proclamation to repentance. Paul exhorted Timothy to preach because "God may perhaps grant them repentance leading to a knowledge of the truth" (1 Tim. 2:25). Repentance is a "turnabout in both thought and action,"[43] so the sermon should "strive to impact the whole person."[44]

The impact upon the total person is vitally important to preachers because the total personality of a human being is how human beings are created in the image of God. Being created in the image of God means that human beings are more than mere machines; furthermore, this means that one's "thinking and feeling should be found together."[45] In other words, the personhood of human beings who listen to sermons each week should be a foremost focus for the pastor as he prepares *and* delivers his sermon. The gospel of Jesus Christ is about life-change (2 Tim. 3:16–17), and pastors must aim to command the congregation under his proclamation to become obedient to the Lord.[46]

---

41. Vines and Shaddix, *Power in the Pulpit*, 315.
42. Vines and Dooley, *Passion in the Pulpit*, 142.
43. Outlaw, "2 Timothy," 335.
44. Allen, *Letters to My Students: On Preaching*, 85.
45. Forlines, *Quest*, 3.
46. Piper, *Brothers, We Are Not Professionals*, 139.

Appendix 1

Paul commands Timothy to continue steadfastly in the ministry to which he has been called by being sober-minded, enduring suffering, doing the work of an evangelist, and fulfilling his ministry (2 Tim. 4:5). Doing these things, of course, is not done by simply showing up to work each day, but by a daily commitment to preparing one's heart to become in tune with God's heart, and then by preaching the Word to those under their care.

The Charge to Preach the Word

It is almost as if Paul is building up to a crescendo for Timothy to hear these next words: "Preach the word; be ready in season and out of season; reprove, rebuke, and exhort, with complete patience and teaching" (2 Tim. 4:2). Within the pastoral epistles, there are three specific reasons why Timothy must preach the Word.

First, preaching is for unbelievers to repent. Paul's words to Timothy and Titus echo the heart of God for His creation—he desires all men to know Him and to come to a knowledge of the truth (1 Tim. 2:3–4). The sole means by which human beings can come to know God is through repentance and faith. Christ's only purpose in coming to this earth was to save sinners, of which Paul claims he was the foremost (1 Tim. 1:15). The reality of preaching the Word of God is that the utmost priority of this task is for sinners to come to Christ through repentance and faith. As David Helm proffers, "We set out to win the hearts of our listeners to the full praise that Christ deserves."[47] The reason for such preaching is because the greatest need for human beings is not a behavioral modification, but a new heart.[48]

Second, preaching is for doctrinal instruction and clarification. Paul not only exhorts Timothy to preach for gospel change, but he also implies that preaching is meant to be instructional. Notice, preaching is not *only* instructional, but instruction is, in fact, a facet of preaching. The Word of God is "profitable for teaching,

---

47. Helm, *Expositional Preaching*, 103.
48. Capill, *The Heart is the Target*, 99.

for reproof, for correction, and for training in righteousness" (2 Tim. 3:16). Köstenberger notes that there are no shortcuts to true spiritual growth[49], which indicates the instructional nature of preaching. The only true way in which pastors can instruct their flock is to rightly handle the Word of truth (2 Tim. 1:15) and to teach sound doctrine (Titus 2:1). Doctrinal instruction and clarification in preaching are necessary because many in the church are confused theologically.

A recent study conducted by *Facts and Trends* concluded that 3 in 10 professing Christians (1 in 5 people polled) claimed that Jesus was a great teacher but was not God; it also found that sixty-five percent of believers are modern-day Arians, believing that Jesus was the first *created* being of God rather than God Himself.[50] Only doctrinal instruction and clarity can "ascertain that the pulpit ministry will challenge the conscience with truthful issues and establish consciences devoid of offense."[51]

Third, preaching is for the believer's sanctification. Forlines posits that one of the goals of Christian preaching is ultimately the sanctification of the congregation, the people of God.[52] Timothy's charge from Paul to preach the Word indicates that the role of the pastor is to equip the saints to navigate the difficult experiences of life through the lens of Christian thought and life. Because preaching is for repentance and because preaching should doctrinally inform and clarify Christian belief, the result of such preaching will be the sanctification of those who already believe.

Conclusion

At the end of the day, the purpose of preaching to make known the glories of God. Pastors do this through several different means, but the most important—and possibly most neglected—means

---

49. Köstenberger, "1–2 Timothy and Titus," 269.
50. Earls, "The Biblical Doctrines Many Evangelicals Get Wrong."
51. Nettles, *The Privilege, Promise, Power, and Peril of Doctrinal Preaching*, 213.
52. Forlines, *Quest*, 240.

is his own heart's preparation and how the heart of the pastor affects his sermon preparation, which then affects the sermon's delivery directly.

Sermon preparation always begins with the pastor's soul. Paul shows Timothy first the principle of self-care before ever encouraging him to enter the study and prepare a sermon. "Train yourself for godliness," Paul writes, "as it holds promise for the present life and also for the life to come" (1 Tim. 4:7–8). In other words, pastors are simply ordinary believers who are called of God to proclaim the gospel to the local body of believers. Pastors are not an elite group of those whom God has given special privileges. No, pastors are simply the called of God to "hold firm to the trustworthy word as taught, so that [they] may be able to give instruction in sound doctrine" (Titus 1:9).

For pastors to adequately prepare their sermons, soul-care is a necessary element of the pastor's daily habits. Rick Reed recalls that the hardest part of his pastoral ministry was what he did with his own heart.[53] Pastors are not only preparing their sermons but are preparing God's Word to be proclaimed from the sacred desk to God's people for salvation and sanctification. Therefore, "we preach not only as heralds but as sinners needing graces"[54] ourselves. Thus, preaching as sinners in need of grace means pastors are inclined to constantly remind themselves that they "were once foolish, disobedient, led astray . . . But when the goodness and loving kindness of God our Savior appeared, he saved us, not because of works done by us in righteousness, but according to his own mercy" (Titus 2:3–5). The message of reconciliation and redemption through mercy and grace fuels the pastor's sermon preparation through the means of his soul care.

Then, as the pastor concludes sermon preparation, he will address the gathering of believers for their spiritual good, but only after preparing himself for the task ahead. Shaddix and Vines propose that for preachers to preach to the heart, they must have a sure calling, a strong personal walk with God, a love for

---

53. Reed, *The Heart of the Preacher*, xv.
54. Capill, *The Heart is the Target*, 248.

"The Role of Spirituality for Sermon Preparation and Delivery"

people, conviction about the great truths of the Bible, and personal heartbreak over their sin and the sins of their hearers.[55] Thus, the delivery of the sermon is the result of the self-care and sermon preparation of the pastor. Sermon delivery is spiritual because God has revealed Himself to us through divine revelation, but it is also spiritual because the pastor transmits God's Word to his congregation in the stead of Christ. Only those who have an intimate union with Him could do as much.

---

55. Vines and Shaddix, *Power in the Pulpit*, 317–19.

Appendix 2

"Addressing Cultural Issues in the Pulpit:
an Essay on Pastors as Public Theologians"

The division of faith and politics can cause a conundrum in a person's mind. It can hinder a person's ability for rational thinking regarding culture and religion, causing questions regarding the distinction and cooperation of faith and politics in the church. These questions stemmed from evangelicals who were worried about the government's oppression over their churches. Thomas Helwys, a leading Baptist theologian, faced these same issues after planting the first Baptist church in England: "However, he also informed the king that they, 'his poor subjects,' intended to be obedient citizens, even to death."[1] Helwys' aim was for the first Baptist church to be "free" from the government's rule, while its members still lived as law-abiding citizens within the country of England.

As centuries passed, the questions of faith and politics and their cooperation became a more significant issue for evangelical churches. No longer is this only about the government controlling what the church can and cannot do, but it is now a question of how believers are to live in a wholly non-Christian world. While

---

1. Estep, "Thomas Helwys: Bold Architect of Baptist Polity on Church-State Relations," 31.

these questions were pervading the minds of evangelicals, certain groups began to formulate their understanding of how to live, as Paul stated, not being conformed to this world, but transformed by renewing our minds (Romans 12:1–2). One radical group of evangelicals believed that the best way they could obey this commandment was to withdraw completely from the culture because of sin's effect on them. Bruce Ashford, formerly associating with such a mindset, notes, "A good Christian should, therefore, withdraw from the evil world and seek a salvation separate from it."[2] This view, along with its strengths, allows for no Christian witness within the culture. Seeking different salvation presents a problem.

Although it is popular to say Christians should be "in the world, but not of the world," David Mathis argues a different point of view. He argues that Jesus' disciples were understandably not to be "of the world," but are to be *sent into* the world. Instead, this should be a mantra for believers. Not only are we to be separate from the world in thought and deed, but also, we are to be sent back into the world to compel others to turn to Christ.[3] The lack of sending is the main weakness of the radical view for withdrawing from culture—Christians are not commanded to do such a thing. Instead, they are commanded to go to the highways and the hedges and compel people to become citizens of the kingdom of God (Luke 14:23). When a believer withdraws from the culture to the degree of having nothing to do within it, there can be no compelling gospel witness. Therefore, the Church must be a beacon of light in the world without withdrawing from the culture around her.

The Church of Jesus Christ is to be a city on a hill (Matt. 5:14). The Almighty God did not establish his church to exist within a world full of sin and be silent, nor did He ordain the communication and formation of His written Word in order that His people would be silent in communicating the truth it contains. Therefore, the Church is a witness to be heard and voiced. Its voice needs to express itself because it is how God's truth communicates in a world full of sinfulness and evil. The reason the Church needs to

---

2. Ashford and Pappalardo, *One Nation Under God*, 16.
3. Mathis, "Let's Revise the Popular Phrase 'In, But Not Of.'"

voice its concerns is because of the massive influence the world has on culture. Too often, the Church is silent in order to be "in the world, but not of the world," while the command is to be ambassadors in the world for Christ and the sake of the gospel message being proclaimed and heard.

Of course, one might question how this plays out in the life of the church. Today's evangelical pulpits have become nothing more than a platform for hot-button issues of the political era in America. Pastors choose to focus much of their preaching time on abortion, homosexuality, and transgenderism, instead of proclaiming the gospel message. Moreover, pastors do need to speak out on such issues, for the Scriptures do the same. However, the more significant question is this: How can pastors be public theologians from their pulpits in a Christ-honoring fashion while maintaining unity in the church? This paper will demonstrate a biblical method will for addressing political issues in the church from the pulpit to serve the people of God well.

The Authority and Inerrancy of Scripture

Os Guinness writes, "Some of today's deadliest challenges to the Christian faith come from within the church itself."[4] For years, the Church has done its worst when speaking out against cultural issues with which the Bible disagrees. Although it is necessary for the Church to speak out against such issues, how she speaks can sometimes be lacking. Often, issues are brought up out of anger and disgust rather than beginning with the Bible and moving forward from there. Believers need to take back what is rightfully theirs: namely, objective moral truth. Each system of government bases its foundational principles on morality taken from Scripture. If this were false, no government could possess any civility; there would be no laws of the land.

Morality is a necessity for civility, but the separation of church and state is also a prerequisite for culture. The Church should *never*

---

4. Guinness, *Fool's Talk*, 210.

influence the government and vice versa. Therefore, the Christian pulpit cannot dictate what the government is to do. John Lewis exclaims, "Moral conscience is needed in order for government and political action to measure up to their divine accountability."[5] Too often, evangelicals operate with the mindset that what their pastor says about political issues should be made into a political campaign. Also, while there is a necessity to speak out against such issues (discussed at length later), there is a prudent way in which to do so.

The Bible is the source of all truth for the believer. In every situation of life, Christians can depend on the Word of God to guide them toward truth, including politics. Isaiah wrote, ". . . so shall my word be that goes out from my mouth; it shall not return to me empty, but it shall accomplish that which I purpose, and shall succeed in the thing for which I sent it" (Isa. 55:11). The Lord has a specific purpose for His Word, and it will complete that which it was sent out to do. This includes the way believers in the twenty-first century treat political ideologies and hot-button issues. This is a weighty point to consider: the Bible contains the truth about right and wrong, and truth must be communicated starting in conservative, evangelical pulpits.

However, until one believes in the inerrancy and infallibility of the Word itself, his proclamation from the sacred desk might as well be insolent talk. The primary, fundamental belief of the pastor who will stand in a pulpit each week must be that the Bible is without error and mistake. God's revelation of Himself is perfectly holy and righteous and truthful. Norman Geisler observes, "No other source equals or surpasses that of Scripture; the Bible, and the Bible alone, is a supremely authoritative book in matters of faith and practice."[6] The Bible is the all-sufficient source for truth and morality, even when it comes to politics and preaching. Each pastor should take rest in the beautiful reality that God has a purpose and knows what he is doing when it comes to the restoration of the

---

5. Lewis, "The Church and the Formation of Political Conscience," 192.
6. Geisler, *Systematic Theology: Introduction and Bible*, 241.

Appendix 2

fallen world. This process begins with a commitment to biblical inerrancy and infallibility.

The preacher should not *only* be committed to the Word of God but also should *apply* it to his foundational methods for proclamation in the pulpit. For many committed evangelicals, the Bible is what they hear preached on Sundays and taught on Wednesdays, and possibly what they read and study personally and with their family throughout the week. However, a disconnect may occur with how the Bible is foundational for *all* speech from the pulpit. They believe that Christianity cannot exist within a culture. Instead, it just exists alongside the culture. Ashford names this view "Grace Alongside Nature."[7] This attitude of cultural engagement essentially claims that while God rules the Church, we should not bring our religion into our political sphere. These two can operate alongside each other without overlapping one another. Typically, this has happened among evangelicals today. There has been a disconnect between faith and politics to a point where the Bible is no longer relevant for our political issues, or we think we should withdraw from all things cultural because it is so full of sin that it cannot bring itself back.

The solution to this problem is to allow the Word of God to be the foundation for all speech in the pulpit. When the Word of God is the basis for all speech in the pulpit, it will permeate throughout our congregations to renew our minds. In speaking of the way Christians can influence culture, Carl F. H. Henry writes, "A single voice that speaks for Jesus in our global conferences can be a determinative voice."[8] Henry is not advocating for a street corner preacher to speak out against hot-button issues and proclaim judgment upon all persons who do not turn from their sin. Instead, he is exhorting believers to understand that to be a Christian is to live in the world as a light for Jesus Christ. Henry claims that believers ought to be the ones going *directly into* the culture to show unbelievers the message of the gospel of grace.[9]

---

7. Ashford, *One Nation Under God*, 19.
8. Henry, *The Uneasy Conscience of Modern Fundamentalism*, 67.
9. Ibid., 71.

The same is true in our pulpits. Therefore, pastors must prepare themselves for how they will represent their churches and the Lord while standing and proclaiming a message behind the sacred desk of the Church of Jesus Christ.

The Pastor as Public Theologian

Henry's observation should probe us pastors to voice Christ from our pulpits with vigor and pride. We preach God's truth as our authority. The pastor is not one who should shy away from cultural issues. Jonah tried to avoid Nineveh at all costs, yet God sovereignly led Jonah back until his obedience was acted out. The same is true for us in America and our churches' pulpits; disengagement is not the answer. Jonathan Leeman said it best, "Cynicism and separation are not options for us."[10] Often, a believer's first response is to withdraw from culture so that it will not influence what is going on within the four walls of the local church. Moreover, this must be a concern for believers, for we do not want our churches to compromise biblical warrants by mimicking culture. Instead, pastors must understand the philosophy of Abraham Kuyper known as sphere sovereignty. Kuyper communicated that "Jesus Christ was Lord over *every* sphere, but he also ordered each sphere according to distinct patterns."[11] Therefore, Christ is also Lord over things, including art, entertainment, politics, and even our churches.

Therefore, pastors cannot digress into their offices and avoid cultural issues and the cultural sphere. Instead, the pastor should use wisdom and prudence to address such issues: "Fearing God is the beginning of wisdom, says Proverbs, and successful political engagement depends on wisdom."[12] Wisdom takes cultural issues into the pulpit and asks, "What is appropriate?" On one hand, the mission of the Church is *not* to address political issues or "fix" the culture (God will redeem culture by his power, not ours). The

---

10. Leeman. *How the Nations Rage*, 163.
11. Ashford, *One Nation Under God*, 28.
12. Leeman, *How the Nations Rage*, 175.

Appendix 2

Church is not in existence to control such things; Kuyper would say politics is a different "sphere."

On the other hand, the Church is not called to be silent on such issues. God placed Joseph in the house of Pharaoh to use him for his glory in Egypt's public square (Gen. 37–39). He placed Esther in the King's palace to free the Jewish people from being destroyed (Esther 4). He also placed Daniel and the three Hebrew children as primary workers for Nebuchadnezzar (Dan. 3). Even Paul used his Roman citizenship to help him appeal his imprisonment (Acts 20–28). These are but a few of the many instances in Scripture showing us that Christians are not to withdraw from culture. However, the Lord has placed preachers in their pulpits "for such a time as this" as well.

In his book *Onward*, Russell Moore gives a hypothetical example of a small church in the Pacific Northwest. Their church was tiny; they did not even have a building in which to gather. One day, a multi-million-dollar business executive walked into their church service to attend a service. Moore proffers that most people would think of all the ways this man could help the church, missionaries, and more. The early church acted a certain way toward the wealthy, and they missed a vitally important aspect of how the Kingdom of God is acted out on earth. He notes that they were lacking in their eschatology and did not have the next trillion years in mind.[13] If pastors are not careful, they can allow political issues to define how they methodize the biblical warrants for how to act as a church. They can allow abortion arguments or marriage debates to rule their speech in the pulpit, which is not the biblical method for preaching.

Therefore, we must not replace preaching with political issues in the pulpit. Part of the problem with the influence of modern evangelicals in the public square is that they are attempting to dictate the political world through biblical monuments on capital lawns and putting prayer back in schools, all while being minimally engaged in culture, if engaged at all. Another issue is the problem of preachers not preaching through Scripture. The radical

---

13. Moore, *Onward*, 81.

fundamentalism that resulted from the Second Great Awakening has played a massive role in this problem of ecclesiasticism—that is, how the "church oversteps its bounds."[14] The church was not created to rule over the government, and vice versa. As Os Guinness writes, "The American republic will be sustained only if each sphere attends to its own purpose in the wider role of society, each is properly checked and balanced, and such principles as subsidiarity are respected."[15] Instead, preachers must address political issues through wisdom and their preaching.

Suggestions for Engaging Culture in the Pulpit

The question of how is where the philosophical becomes practical. Although many of the topics addressed early on in this paper could be taken as irrelevant, we must build a foundation to get to this place in the argument. Until this point, the argument has been for the Christian, specifically the preacher, to use the Word of God as his foundation and his authority, and to use wisdom and prudence to address issues of the culture in the pulpit. However, the most critical element of this philosophy is that the preacher will not allow these types of issues to replace the preaching of the Word of God each week. So what follows are a few practical suggestions for the preacher to do what he is called to do (preach), and to help him form a method of addressing cultural issues from the pulpit when necessary.

Preach Expository Sermons

Many conversations are going on within evangelical circles regarding the method by which preachers use to proclaim the message of Jesus Christ each week. It is no surprise to anyone to see different methods of preaching used in the pulpit. However, the essential approach for preachers to address cultural issues is for them to

---

14. Ashford. *Letter to an American Christian*, 43.
15. Guinness, *A Free People's Suicide*, 195.

preach expository sermons. Many pastors and scholars would define expository sermons in a multitude of ways; however, Hershael York has a simple, yet practical definition: "Expository preaching is any kind of preaching that shows people the meaning of a text and leads them to apply it to their lives."[16] Often, a preacher's definition of what preaching is contains many different elements and it confuses the audience. York's definition of expository preaching gets to the heart of expository preaching: interpreting a text that invokes application.

Application allows preachers to address cultural issues. Expository preaching is not merely a "step-by-step method" to address cultural issues. Instead, it allows the preacher the opportunity to give authority to the Scriptures while he is preaching. Too often, churches and pastors believe that it is their job to address specific "issues" and receive "Amens" from a particular corner of their sanctuaries. However, Moore observes that Jesus "never turned the sword of the Spirit into a security blanket for the already convinced."[17] This method has become a staple mantra for evangelical churches. It is all too easy for believers (especially pastors) to address outsiders and condemn them for *where they are living their lives sinfully*. However, this is not the method Jesus used, nor should it be our method. Our method should be to show them their lack of righteousness and holiness, and we do so by interpreting a text of Scripture and appealing to our hearers week after week.

Allow the Bible to Speak for Itself

The Bible does not need our help with relation to addressing any issue, specifically cultural ones. Instead, the preacher should look to the Bible as his sole authority in the pulpit. The Bible, according to the author of Hebrews, is "living and active, sharper than any two-edged sword, piercing to the division of soul and of spirit,

---

16. York and Decker, *Preaching with Bold Assurance*, 33.
17. Moore, *Onward*, 198.

of joints and of marrow, and discerning the thoughts and intentions of the heart" (Heb. 4:12). The Bible is sufficient, relevant, and powerful enough to engage with culture at any time. Therefore, the pastor should rest on the foundational truth that the Bible is sufficient to speak for itself. God does not need preachers to help address cultural issues. Instead, the pastor, while preaching expository sermons, can allow the Bible to speak on its authority and with its power. The pastor is nothing more than a conduit through which the message is given. John Stott writes on crossing cultural barriers in preaching; instead of being a zeitgeist, we should be determined to build our bridge from church to culture based on the Bible.[18] The way to build our bridge and address culture is by allowing the Bible to speak for itself. Kevin DeYoung says it best: "I want my people to expect, that as a general rule, the Bible sets the agenda not my interests or what I think is relevant."[19]

Do Not Allow Personal Interpretation to Override What the Bible Means to Say

As preachers, we cannot merely approach cultural issues in America and place a biblical passage on its rhetoric and call it a sermon. York exclaims that we are not at liberty to tell a bank our understanding for a mortgage means that we do not have to make a payment each month.[20] The same is true in the way we preach. There is one meaning of a particular text that can be made manifest in many different applications. That there are many different applications of one text does not indicate more than one *original* meaning. The Word of God is relevant to all life and spans generation after generation; this can result in many different forms of application but does not change the intended meaning of a particular passage. Therefore, it is not sufficient for a pastor to stand in the pulpit and claim 2 Chronicles 7:14 as the church's statement

---

18. Stott, *Between Two Worlds*, 139.
19. DeYoung, "The Preacher and Politics: Seven Thoughts."
20. York and Decker, *Preaching with Bold Assurance*, 30.

of revival for America. Instead, he must allow the biblical text to dictate how he presents the application of such a passage within the context of modern America.

Allowing the original intended meaning of a text to be the foundation for application is one major focal point of expository preaching. When a pastor is preaching expository sermons, he is already allowing the biblical text to be the foundation and the sole source for the sermon. Therefore, it continues to afford the preacher liberty to preach with confidence because he is proclaiming "Thus saith the Lord."

Use the Holy Spirit's Guidance to Address Cultural Issues

Ultimately, the Holy Spirit must be the guide for a pastor when it comes to addressing cultural issues from the pulpit. Yes, expository sermons will allow the pastor to address issues *as he preaches*. However, sometimes, current events will necessitate a response from a pastor. Jonathan Leeman defines this process as *principled pragmatism*. Principled pragmatism says that we should use wisdom to do justice: " We must start by asking God what *he* intends for us and for the world, lest we let some other god set the terms."[21] Mainly, Leeman's approach takes the good from all forms of politics—liberalism, conservatism, and nationalism—and leaves the bad. We can do the same in our pulpits. Take the good from cultural issues and leave the bad. Of course, we must *always* expose sin and evil for what it is, yet we can still do so in a loving, Christ-centered manner.

Conclusion

Pastors need a methodical approach to addressing cultural issues in the pulpit. The church is not the place to fix cultural problems—we have a public square for that purpose. However, the church can be a means through which God can reveal his truth and transform

---

21. Leeman, *How the Nations Rage*, 181.

culture. Carl F. H. Henry writes, "The implications of this for evangelicalism seem clear. The battle against evil in all its forms must be pressed unsparingly; we must pursue the enemy, in politics, in economics, in science in ethics—everywhere, in every field, we must pursue relentlessly."[22] To do this, pastors must preach expository sermons. The expository sermon takes the text and interprets its original meaning and then applies it to the hearers' lives. However, expository sermons also allow the Bible to do its bidding. No longer does the pastor have to depend upon his intellect or personality to address cultural issues because the Bible can speak for itself.

Another aspect of addressing cultural issues is that preachers do not have to try and make up an interpretation when they preach the Bible. Instead, they can allow the Bible to mean what it intends to mean and communicate it with power and authority. The pastor cannot do any of these things without the consideration of the Holy Spirit's guidance in their life.

Nevertheless, Christians are not to withdraw from culture. The answer, of course, is not withdrawing. Instead, Richard Mouw argues that Christians have a mandate (Gen. 1:28) from the Lord to live within the culture. He writes, "This cultural mandate is an expression of God's own investment in cultural formation, and it has in no way been canceled by the introduction of sin into the creation."[23] Our cultural interaction is not null and void because of the fall. If anything, it has been heightened because of how God aims to redeem creation and culture. Therefore, it is imperative for pastors to stay up to date on current events, but they should use discretion when addressing such things.

---

22. Henry, *The Uneasy Conscience of Modern Fundamentalism*, 86.
23. Mouw, *The Challenges of Cultural Discipleship*, 41.

Bibliography

Affleck, Bert. "John Wesley's Spiritual Disciplines for Today's Pastor" *Perkin's Journal* 40, no 1, (Jan.: 1987), 1-8.
Allen, Jason K. *Letters to My Students: On* Preaching. Nashville: B&H, 2019.
Allen, Lewis. *The Preacher's* Catechism. Wheaton: Crossway, 2018.
Allen, Wesley O Jr. "An Hour of Study: Sermon Preparation as a Spiritual Discipline" *Lexington Theological Quarterly* 45, no 1, (Spr.- Sum.: 2013), 17-35.
Bauermeister, Paul J. "The Disciplines of Pastoral Formation: Habits Toward Holiness" *Currents in Theology and Mission* 15, no 1 (Feb. 1988), 62-67.
Beeke, Joel R. *Reformed Preaching: Proclaiming God's Word from the Heart of the Preacher to the Heart of His People.* Wheaton: Crossway, 2018.
Beeke, Joel R., and Dustin Benge. *Pulpit Aflame: Essays in Honor of Steven J. Lawson.* Grand Rapids: Reformation Heritage Books, 2016.
Bracey, Matthew Steven and W. Jackson Watts. *The Promise of Arminian Theology: Essays in Honor of F. Leroy Forlines.* Nashville: Randall House, 2016.
Bridges, Charles. *The Christian* Ministry. Edinburgh: Banner of Truth Trust, 1967.
Bridges, Jerry. *The Discipline of Grace: God's Role and Our Role in the Pursuit of Holiness.* Colorado Springs: NavPress, 2006.
Calvin, John. *Institutes of the Christian Religion*, trans. Henry Beveridge. Peabody, Mass.: Hendrickson, 2008.
Capill, Murray. *The Heart is the Target: Preaching Practical Application from Every* Text. Phillipsburg: P&R, 2014.
Carson, Donald A. "Spiritual Disciplines" *Themelios* 36, no 3 (Nov. 2011), 377-79.
———. *A Call to Spiritual Reformation: Priorities from Paul and His Prayers.* Grand Rapids: Baker, 1992.
Chapell, Bryan. *Christ-Centered Preaching: Redeeming the Expository Sermon.* Grand Rapids: Baker Academic, 1994.
Charles, H.B. *On Pastoring: A Short Guide to Living, Leading, and Ministering as A Pastor.* Chicago: Moody, 2016.
Christian Standard Bible. Nashville: Holman Bible Publishers, 2017.

Bibliography

Corn, Randy. "A Few Borrowed Words About Plagiarism." *Free Will Baptist Theology,* accessed December 9, 2019, https://www.fwbtheology.com/a-few-borrowed-words-about-plagiarism/.

Dever, Mark. *Discipling: Helping Others Follow Christ.* Wheaton: Crossway, 2016.

———. *The Gospel and Personal Evangelism.* Wheaton: Crossway, 2007.

Mark Dever and Paul Alexander. *The Deliberate Church: Building Your Ministry on the Gospel* (Wheaton: Crossway, 2005), 36.

Dockery, David S. *Theology, Church, and Ministry: A Handbook for Theological Education.* Nashville: B&H Academic, 2017.

Doriani, Dan. "Preach in a Mild State of Panic." *The Gospel Coalition,* accessed September 21, 2019, https://www.thegospelcoalition.org/article/preach-in-a-mild-state-of-panic/.

Duhigg, Charles. *The Power of Habit: Why We Do What We Do in Life and Business.* New York: Random House, 2014.

Emmert, Kevin. "Resting in the Word of God: The Forgotten Spiritual Discipline." *Christianity Today* 56, no 3 (March 2012), 36–37.

English Standard Version. Wheaton: Crossway, 2001.

Farrell, Hobert K. "Preach, Proclaim," in *Evangelical Dictionary of Biblical Theology,* electronic ed., Baker Reference Library. Grand Rapids: Baker Book House, 1996.

Ferguson, Sinclair B. *Devoted to God: Blueprints for Sanctification.* Edinburgh: Banner of Truth Trust, 2016.

———. *Maturity: Growing Up and Going On in the Christian Life.* Edinburgh: Banner of Truth, 2019.

———. *The Whole Christ: Legalism, Antinomianism, & Gospel Assurances—Why the Marrow Controversy Still Matters.* Wheaton: Crossway, 2016.

Fernando, Ajith. *The Family Life of a Christian Leader.* Wheaton: Crossway, 2016.

Freeman, Carroll B. "The Spiritual Disciplines in Personal Formation." *The Theological Educator* 43 (Spring: 1991), 91–97.

Forlines, F. Leroy. *Biblical Ethics.* Nashville: Randall House, 1973.

———. *The Quest for Truth: Theology for Postmodern Times.* Nashville: Randall House, 2001.

Frame, John M. *The Doctrine of the Word of God.* Phillipsburg: P&R, 2010.

———. *The Doctrine of the Knowledge of God.* Phillipsburg: P&R Publishing, 1987.

Geisler, Norman L., "Introduction and Bible" vol. 1 in *Systematic Theology.* Minneapolis: Bethany House, 2002.

Gibson, Scott M. "The Preacher's Personal World" in *The Worlds of the Preacher: Navigating Biblical, Cultural, and Personal Contexts.* Grand Rapids: Baker Academic, 2018.

———. *Should We Use Someone Else's Sermon?: Preaching in a Cut-and-Paste World.* Grand Rapids: Zondervan, 2008.

Bibliography

Guthrie, Donald. *"Pastoral Epistles: An Introduction and Commentary,"* vol. 14, *Tyndale New Testament Commentaries*. Downers Grove, IL: InterVarsity, 1990.

Hardin, Leslie T. "The Quest for the Spiritual Jesus: Jesus and the Spiritual Disciplines" *Stone Campbell Journal* 15, no 2, (Fall 2012), 217–27.

Harrod, Joseph C. "Knowing God from the Heart: Samuel Davies and the Means of Grace" *Puritan Reformed Journal*, 6 no 2 (July 2014), 216–57.

Hughes, R. Kent. *Disciplines of a Godly Man* Wheaton: Crossway, 2001.

———. "The Preacher's Toolkit: How Do I Prepare My Heart to Preach?" *The Gospel Coalition*, accessed December 17, 2019, https://www.thegospelcoalition.org/article/preachers-toolkit-how-do-i-prepare-my-heart-to-preach/.

Köstenberger, Andreas J., *Biblical Theology for Christian Proclamation: Commentary on 1–2 Timothy and Titus*, ed. T. Desmond Alexander, Andreas J. Köstenberger, and Thomas R. Schreiner. Nashville: B&H, 2017.

Hull, Robert W. *Conversion and Discipleship: You Can't Have One Without the Other*. Grand Rapids: Zondervan, 2016.

Keller, Timothy. *Preaching: Communicating Faith in an Age of Skepticism*. New York: Viking Press, 2015.

Lawson, Steven J. *The Kind of Preaching God Blesses*. Eugene, OR: Harvest House, 2013.

———. "Preparing the Pastor" *Expositor Magazine*, accessed August 9, 2019, https://www.expositormagazine.org/new-blog/2018/4/12/preparing-the-pastor.

Lewis, C.S. *Mere Christianity*. Nashville: Harper Collins, 1952.

Liddell, Henry George. *A Greek-English Lexicon*. Oxford: Clarendon Press, 1996.

Lloyd-Jones, Martyn D. *Preaching and Preachers*, 40th Anniversary Edition. Grand Rapids: Zondervan, 2011.

MacArthur, John Jr. *Rediscovering Expository Preaching*. Nashville: Thomas Nelson, 1992.

———. "1 Corinthians," *The MacArthur New Testament Commentary*. Chicago: Moody, 1984.

McGrath, Alister E. *Mere Discipleship: Growing in Wisdom and Hope*. Grand Rapids: Baker, 2018.

Meuer, Siegfreid. "What is Biblical Preaching: Exegesis and Meditation for the Sermon" *Encounter* 24, no 2 (Spr. 1963), 182–89.

Morgan, Robert J. *Reclaiming the Lost Art of Biblical Meditation: Find True Peace in Jesus*. Nashville: Thomas Nelson, 2017.

Nash, Ronald H. *Life's Ultimate Questions: An Introduction to Philosophy*. Grand Rapids: Zondervan, 1999.

Nettles, Thomas J. *The Privilege, Promise, Power, and Peril of Doctrinal Preaching*. Greenbrier, AR: Free Grace Press, 2018.

Pace, Scott R. *Preaching by the Book: Developing and Delivering Text-Driven Sermons*. Nashville: B&H Academic, 2018.

Bibliography

Packer, J.I. *Keep in Step with the Spirit: Finding Fulfillment in Our Walk with God*. Grand Rapids: Baker, 2005.

———. *Evangelism and the Sovereignty of God*. Downers Grove: InterVarsity, 2008.

"Pastor's Long Work Hours Come at Expense of People, Ministry" *LifeWay Research*, accessed December 16, 2019, https://lifewayresearch.com/2010/01/05/pastors-long-work-hours-come-at-expense-of-people-ministry/.

Peterson Eugene, *The Message*. Colorado Springs: NavPress, 2002.

Phillips, John, "Psalms 89–150" vol. 2 in *Exploring the Psalms*. Phillipsburg: P&R, 1988.

Picirilli, Robert E. *Teacher, Leader, Shepherd: The New Testament Pastor*. Nashville: Randall House, 2007.

———. "1,2 Corinthians" in *The Randall House Bible Commentary*. Nashville: Randall House, 1987.

Pierce, Timothy M. *Enthroned on Our Praise: An Old Testament Theology of Worship*. Nashville: B&H, 2008.

Pink, Arthur, W. *Spiritual Growth: Growth in Grace, or Christian Progress*. Ann Arbor, MI: Cushing-Alloy, 1972.

Pinson, J. Matthew. *Perspectives on Christian Worship: 5 Views*. Nashville: B&H Academic, 2009.

Piper, John. *A Peculiar Glory: How the Christian Scriptures Reveal Their Complete Truthfulness*. Wheaton: Crossway, 2016.

———. *Brothers, We Are Not Professionals: A Plea to Pastors for Radical Ministry*. Nashville: B&H, 2013.

———. *Expository Exultation: Christian Preaching as Worship*. Wheaton: Crossway, 2018.

———. *The Pleasures of God: Meditations of God's Delight in Being God*. Sisters, OR: Multnomah, 2000.

———. *Reading the Bible Supernaturally: Seeing and Savoring the Glory of God in Scripture*. Wheaton: Crossway, 2017.

Plantinga, Alvin. *Knowledge and Christian Belief*. Grand Rapids: Eerdmans, 2015.

Plummer, Robert L. "Are the Spiritual Disciplines of 'Silence and Solitude' Really Biblical?" *Journal of Spiritual Formation and Soul Care* 2, no 1, (Spring 2009), 101–12.

"Reasons for Attrition Among Pastors," *LifeWay Research*, accessed November 29, 2019, http://lifewayresearch.com/wp-content/uploads/2015/08/Reasons-for-Attrition-Among-Pastors-Quantitative-Report-Final1.pdf.

Reed, Oscar F. "Hosea" in *The Beacon Bible Commentary: Hosea through Malachi*. Kansas City, Mo.: Beacon Hill, 1966.

Reed, Rick. *The Heart of the Preacher: Preparing Your Soul to Proclaim the Word of God*. Bellingham: Lexham Press, 2019.

Robinson, Haddon W. *Biblical Preaching: The Development and Delivery of Expository Messages*. Grand Rapids: Baker, 1980.

Sanders, Oswald J. *Spiritual Maturity*. Chicago: Moody, 1994.

Bibliography

———. *Spiritual Leadership: Principles of Excellence for Every Believer.* Chicago: Moody, 2007.

Schreiner, Thomas R., "Commentary on Hebrews" in *Biblical Theology for Christian Proclamation*, ed. T. Desmond Alexander, Andreas J. Köstenberger, and Thomas R. Schreiner. Nashville: B&H, 2015.

Smethurst, Matt. *Before You Open Your Bible: Nine Heart Postures for Approaching God's Word.* Leyland, England: 10Publishing, 2019.

Smith, John E., "Religious Affections" vol. 2 in *The Works of Jonathan Edwards.* New Haven: Yale University Press, 1959.

Southeastern Seminary, "Mike Glenn—The Marathon of Ministry—1 Kings 19:1–8" *YouTube.* Online Video Clip, https://www.youtube.com/watch?v=DURkQMrMxJo&t=1s.

Spurgeon, C.H. *Lectures to My Students.* Grand Rapids: Zondervan, 1954.

———. "The Infallibility of Scripture," *Spurgeon Gems*, accessed December 9, 2019, https://www.spurgeongems.org/vols34-36/chs2013.pdf.

Stott, John R.W. *Between Two Worlds: The Art of Preaching in the Twentieth Century.* Grand Rapids: Eerdmans, 1982.

Swanson, James, *Dictionary of Biblical Languages with Semantic Domains: Hebrew (Old Testament)* (Oak Harbor: Logos Research Systems, Inc., 1997).

"The Place of Biblical Theology" *The Old Testament Student*, Vol. 3, no. 6 (Feb. 1884), 200–201.

Tripp, Paul David. *Dangerous Calling: Confronting the Unique Challenges of Pastoral Ministry.* Wheaton: Crossway, 2012.

Vanhoozer, Kevin J. "Lost in Interpretation? Truth, Scripture, and Hermeneutics" *JETS* no. 48 vol. 1 (March 2005), 89–114.

Vines, Jerry and Jim Shaddix. *Power in the Pulpit: How to Prepare and Deliver Expository Sermons.* Chicago: Moody, 2017.

Wells, David F. *The Courage to Be Protestant: Truth-lovers, Marketers, and Emergents in the Postmodern World.* Grand Rapids: Eerdmans, 2008.

Whitney, Donald S. *Spiritual Disciplines for the Christian Life.* Colorado Springs: NavPress, 2014.

———. *Ten Questions to Diagnose Your Spiritual Health.* Colorado Springs: NavPress, 2001.

Willard, Dallas. "Spiritual Disciplines, Spiritual Formation, and the Restoration of the Soul" *Journal of Psychology and Theology* 26, no. 1, (Spring 1998), 101–9.

Wilson, Jared C. *The Pastor's Justification: Applying the Work of Christ into Your Life and Ministry.* Wheaton: Crossway, 2013.

Winner, Lauren F. "Preaching as a Spiritual Discipline" *Sewanee Theological Review* 57, no 4 (Michaelmas 2014), 517–26.

Yoder, June A. "The Sermon as Fulcrum: The Role of Preaching in Worship" *Vision* 10, no. 1 (Spring 2009), 36–42.

York, Hershael, and Bert Decker. *Preaching with Bold Assurance: A Solid and Enduring Approach to Engaging Exposition.* Nashville: B&H, 2003.

Zuck, Roy B. *Basic Bible Interpretation: A Practical Guide to Discovering Biblical Truth.* Colorado Springs: Victor, 1991.

www.ingramcontent.com/pod-product-compliance
Lightning Source LLC
Chambersburg PA
CBHW070454090426
42735CB00012B/2553